THE
HUMAN
STORY

OUR EVOLUTION
FROM PREHISTORIC
ANCESTORS to TODAY

CHRISTOPHER SLOAN

FOREWORD BY

DR. MEAVE LEAKEY AND DR. LOUISE LEAKEY

PHOTOGRAPHY BY KENNETH GARRETT   ART BY KENNIS AND KENNIS

NATIONAL GEOGRAPHIC
WASHINGTON, D.C.

Published by the National Geographic Society
1145 17th St. N.W.
Washington, D.C., 20036-4688

John M. Fahey
President and Chief Executive Officer

Gilbert M. Grosvenor
Chairman of the Board

Nina D. Hoffman
*Executive Vice President and
President, Books and
Education Publishing Group*

Ericka Markman
*Senior Vice President and President,
Children's Books and Education
Publishing Group*

Staff for this book

Nancy Laties Feresten
*Vice President and Editor-in-Chief,
Children's Books
Project Editor*

Bea Jackson
Art Director, Children's Books

Lewis R. Bassford
Production Manager

Vincent Ryan
Manufacturing Manager

Julia Marshall
Indexer

Design by Christopher Sloan

Principal Consultants

Dr. Susan Antón
Associate Professor of Anthropology
Rutgers University

Dr. Meave Leakey
Research Affiliate
National Museums of Kenya

Dr. Louise Leakey
Research Scientist
National Museums of Kenya

Dr. Eric Meikle
Outreach Coordinator
National Center for Science Education

Dr. Richard Potts
Director, Human Origins Project
Smithsonian Institution

Special advisors

Early hominids
Dr. Zeresenay Alemseged
Institute of Human Origins at
Arizona State University

Genetics
Dr. John Relethford
State University of New York
at Oneonta

Tools and archaeology
Dr. John J. Shea
State University of New York
at Stony Brook

Neandertals and modern humans
Dr. Erella Hovers
Institute of Archaeology
The Hebrew University

Acknowledgments

I have had the pleasure of working with many
talented and inspiring colleagues at NATIONAL
GEOGRAPHIC MAGAZINE. Among them,
Illustrations Editor Elie Rogers, Science Editor
Rick Gore, and photographer Ken Garrett stand
out as three collaborators who shared my
enthusiasm for paleoanthropology. Together we
spent many hours with countless scientists
discussing ideas that led to the creation of many
magazine articles and eventually, this book. So,
I thank them and the many paleoanthropologists
who guided us through this difficult subject and
shared their insights so graciously. I also thank
Jill Burch for helping me collect images for this
book and my family for sustaining their support
for my work on this project over many months.
Special thanks to Dr. Jonathan Marks for his
help with genetic distances on page 11, Dr.
Alison Brooks for her help with the map on page
64, Dr. William Kimbel for the photo on page
28, and Dr. David Lordkipanidze for the photo
on page 38. Finally, I'd like to acknowledge the
staff of the National Geographic Society's
Children's Book Division for being so helpful
on this project.

Illustration credits:

All photography by Kenneth Garrett and all
artwork by Alfons Kennis and Adrie Kennis
except as credited otherwise throughout the
book. The Kennis brothers' illustrations first
appeared in *De Oermens* published by Uitgeverij
Leopold bv, Amsterdam, Netherlands.

Cover: Neandertal by Kennis and Kennis
Back cover: Bonobo by Kennis and Kennis,
photo by Kenneth Garrett

Library of Congress
Cataloging-in-Publication Data
available on request.

ISBN: 0-7922-6325-1

Printed in Belgium

**Many of the features we humans take for granted, such as
having five fingers and toes, a set of baby and adult teeth,
and hair, evolved among early mammal-like animals, such as
Sinoconodon (left), which lived 200 million years ago.**

Contents

Homo heidelbergensis (right) is one of as many as three kinds of human ancestors that lived 500,000 years ago.

Foreword

Humans are innately curious about their origins. Fortunately our ancestors left clues that tell us about our past in fossil and archaeological sites around the world. By searching for these clues and by comparing the fossils and stone tools that we find, we can begin to tell the fascinating story of how we became human.

Our family—the Leakeys—has been involved in this search for over 70 years, and we continue the search today, focusing on the rich fossil beds of the great Rift Valley in East Africa. The story this book tells has been drawn from fossils of human ancestors found by the Leakey family digs and by numerous other digs all over the world.

It is six million years since our earliest ancestors, the first apes that walked upright, emerged. Our own species, *Homo sapiens*, has lived on this Earth only 200,000 years. In that short time our species has used its large and intelligent brain to develop complex technology, which has allowed us today to dominate and change the planet in which we live.

This dominance comes at a price. Because we are destructive, because we want to change the planet on which we depend, and because we have a strong desire to own places and things, we increasingly threaten the world in which we live. But because of our superior intelligence, we have the ability to direct the course of our own and our planet's future to the benefit of all.

In this book, Christopher Sloan teaches us about the history we all share. We are the only surviving hominin, and we all have a common African origin and a common future. Every individual must play his or her part in securing this future not only for our own species, but also for all those species with whom we have the privilege to share this fragile Earth.

Kenyanthropus (above), was a human ancestor that lived between 3.5 and 3.2 million years ago in Africa. Many similar bones and other evidence, such as the ancient footprints being studied at Laetoli in Tanzania (left), suggest that Africa is where the human story began.

Dr. Meave Leakey and Dr. Louise Leakey
Explorers-in-Residence, National Geographic Society
Kenya, April 2003

CHAPTER ONE

OF BONES & GENES

What is a human being? Is it a creature that walks, talks, and paints pictures? Sure, but scientists who study how we became human see no single moment in time to point to and say, "That's when we became human." Instead, they see that everything that makes us different from other animals appeared in our ancestors at different times over millions of years. Some things, such as the great flexibility of our shoulder joints, had their origins as far back as 125 million years ago. Having really big brains, on the other hand, is only a few hundred thousand years old. The human we see in today's mirror is like a mosaic of many tiles, some extremely old and some very new.

Humans share much of their history with the great apes: orangutans, gorillas, and chimpanzees. Scientists reported on the similarities of human and chimpanzee anatomy over three hundred years ago, but set humans apart as a group. More recently, studies of the genome, the set of instructions in each cell that tells an organism how to function and grow, have shown that the chimpanzee genome may differ from the human genome by only five percent or even less. This would make chimpanzees more closely related to humans than to gorillas.

This surprising picture is the result of scientists knowing more about how organisms change over time than they did in the past. And knowing more is why it is difficult today to define exactly what a human is. For the purposes of this book, however, all of our ancestors back to the point where we shared a common ancestor with chimpanzees 6 million years ago will be called "human."

Neandertals, such as the one shown at far right, were among the first human ancestors to be recognized as a different kind of human. Shown in the background are a Neandertal jawbone and a skull (above). At near right are their stone tools. These were different from the tools most often found with the remains of modern humans.

The genetic code, or genome, that controls how we grow and how our bodies function is contained in the **DNA** within the chromosome pairs inside each cell's nucleus (see diagram below).

At right is a map of Chromosome 17. This is just one example of how scientists have identified the locations of many genes that can play a role in diseases from cancers to mental illness.

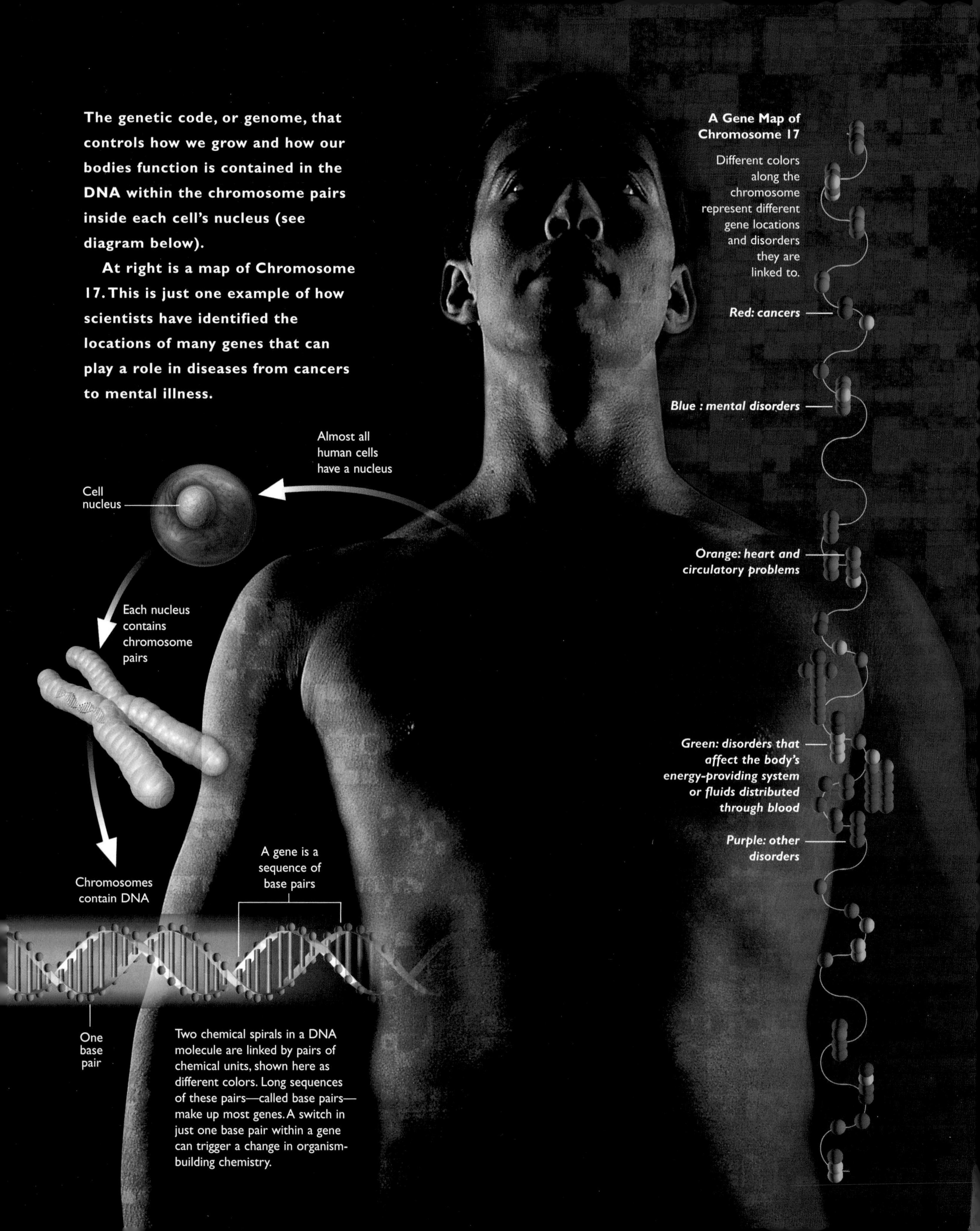

A Gene Map of Chromosome 17

Different colors along the chromosome represent different gene locations and disorders they are linked to.

Red: cancers —

Blue : mental disorders —

Orange: heart and circulatory problems —

Green: disorders that affect the body's energy-providing system or fluids distributed through blood —

Purple: other disorders —

Almost all human cells have a nucleus

Cell nucleus —

Each nucleus contains chromosome pairs

Chromosomes contain DNA

A gene is a sequence of base pairs

One base pair

Two chemical spirals in a DNA molecule are linked by pairs of chemical units, shown here as different colors. Long sequences of these pairs—called base pairs—make up most genes. A switch in just one base pair within a gene can trigger a change in organism-building chemistry.

Yet many of these humans did not look like us. Many kinds probably looked more like apes. It was only around 100,000 years ago that we humans evolved our current body form.

Yet a body like ours is still not enough to define what a human is today. This is because an important part of what makes us human is a set of behaviors we share as a species. This modern behavior includes the ability to think abstractly (about things that are not real, for example), to make complex plans, to be creative and innovative, and to use symbols—such as the written word.

There is debate among scientists about how and when our ancestors began to behave in this modern way. Some scientists see it as a gradual process that occurred over hundreds of thousands of years. Others see evidence of an abrupt change in behavior around 50,000 years ago. However and whenever this modern behavior emerged, it is clear that it led to the elaborate communication, culture, and technology that allows us to live virtually anywhere we please today.

All of the stages of being human are the result of evolution. Evolution is defined as the genetic change that living things experience over many generations that results in the appearance of new species. Evidence of these changes can be found in the genome.

Every living thing has a different genome. While the basic genomes of all elephants contain the instructions for growing trunks and tusks, each elephant also has its own *individual* genome. This is what makes each one a male or female, slightly larger or smaller, and so on. Likewise, all humans share the basic genome needed to grow arms, legs, fingers, and toes, but each of us also has our own individual genome that gives us our particular hair and skin color, height, sex, and many other characteristics.

Genomes change over time. In some cases changes occur that are major enough that they result in new species. All whales, for example, evolved from four-legged land-dwelling animals distantly related to hippos. And birds evolved from dinosaurs. Changing genomes are not only responsible for the variety of life on Earth today, but for all of the different forms of life that lived in the past.

In the last few decades, scientists have made great progress in understanding genomes. We know that each genome is made of long strings of chemical combinations

The similar genomes of humans and chimpanzees suggest we shared a common ancestor about six million years ago. Fossil evidence and the behavior of living primates, including humans, give clues to what that creature looked like and how it might have behaved.

9

WE ARE ALL MUTANTS

Evolutionary changes in living things are possible because of mutations. Mutated monsters are Hollywood's version of mutations, but in nature genetic change by mutation is frequent and completely normal. Most mutations are simply accidental copying mistakes made when the billions of base pairs in the DNA of parents are being combined to produce offspring. Most of these mistakes go completely unnoticed because they have no effect on appearance or bodily functions. In fact, much of our genetic material is called "junk DNA" because it has no known function. Mutations that do affect appearance or bodily functions, however, impact the evolution of an organism because they create new genetic versions—or variants—of organisms. These variations play a key role in **natural selection**.

Natural selection is the process that influences whether or not an organism reproduces. If a mutation creates a variant of an animal or plant that makes it healthier and stronger, this might improve its ability to survive in an environment and reproduce. It would then have a chance to pass its genes—perhaps including the mutation—on to its offspring.

Mutations can also make variants of animals and plants that are more likely to be selected as mates. This influences **sexual selection**. Many female birds, for example, are attracted to males with bright colored feathers, which can be a sign of good health. As a result, mutations that influence feather color can affect the mating success of male birds.

Over time, natural selection, with sexual selection as an important part, can result in physical or behavioral changes within a whole group of organisms. Given enough time, they can also result in changes that produce completely new species.

A recent study showed how a single mutation is responsible for creating increased surface area of the cerebral cortex in mice brains. This created more folding of brain tissue in mice with the mutation (left) than in those without (right). In humans, the cerebral cortex is associated with reading, writing, and solving intricate problems. This part of the brain in primates, especially humans, expanded greatly during evolution.

CROSS-SECTIONS
OF MICE HEADS
ARE NOT TO SCALE

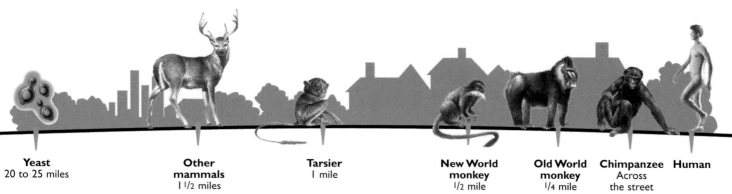

Yeast	Other mammals	Tarsier	New World monkey	Old World monkey	Chimpanzee	Human
20 to 25 miles	1 1/2 miles	1 mile	1/2 mile	1/4 mile	Across the street	

The amount of genetic difference between us and other animals can be looked at as the genetic distance between us and our common ancestor with that animal. To give a rough idea of how closely related we are to other organisms, here is a depiction of our genetic "neighborhood." If yeast were 25 miles distant from humans, all mammals would be within 1 1/2 miles, and chimpanzees would live across the street.

called DNA molecules. These molecules are made of chemical units that pair up and arrange themselves into a pair of spiraling chemical strings called a double helix. Specific sequences of paired chemical units—or base pairs—along the strings are called "genes" *(see page 8)*.

The first organisms whose genomes were studied were single-celled organisms such as yeast. Yeast was found to have 12 million base pairs and over 6,000 identifiable genes along its DNA. The genomes of round worms, mosquitoes, mice, and even humans have since been added to the list of genomes that have been recorded. The human genome has more than three billion base pairs, and along its spiraling DNA molecules are approximately 30,000 genes.

By looking at similarities between the genomes in different organisms, scientists can determine how closely animals are related. Yeast seems like it should be very distant from us, but it actually has genes that are identical to some found in humans. This implies that long ago yeast and humans shared a common ancestor. Since yeast, a very simple organism, has similar genes to humans, one would predict that other animals more complex than yeast share even more genes with humans. This turns out to be true. All mammals, whether cheetahs or mice, share much of their genetic material with humans because all mammals share a mammalian common ancestor that lived back in the time of dinosaurs.

Our understanding of relationships among animals, including ourselves, began long before the development of genetic science. In 1735, a Swedish scientist named Carolus Linnaeus came up with a system for categorizing and naming all known animals and plants—including humans—using anatomical and structural differences. Linnaeus saw that the shape of our bones and the way our skeletons fit together are similar to what can be seen in apes and apelike creatures. So he placed humans, apes, monkeys, and lemurs in the same order, primates, which means "first."

The system of Linnaeus *(see page 14)* established the obvious relationships among living things, but he did not try to explain how they got that way. That was left to other scientists who viewed the concept of evolution as a possible explanation. The idea that plants and animals changed through successive generations into different forms had been discussed among scientists for many years, but no one could say exactly how it worked. It took another hundred years beyond the time of Linnaeus before a theory emerged that could explain the evolution of humans, indeed all life, in scientific terms. This was accomplished by 19th century British scientists Charles Darwin and Alfred Russel Wallace.

Both Darwin and Wallace had travelled the world and observed that plants and animals were often ideally suited for certain lifestyles or environments. They noticed how limited resources and environmental change could dramatically affect species. A single event, such as a drought, could cause whole groups of animals and plants to be wiped out very quickly. At the same time another group could thrive. Some animals and plants might survive to reproduce. Others might not.

Why was this? One reason is that different variations of plants and animals may have an advantage—or a disadvantage—depending on the environment or conditions they are in. It is this variation in plants and animals that provides the genetic grist for the mill of evolutionary change. When one variant reproduces more than another, for whatever reason, the chances that its traits will be passed on to succeeding generations are increased. Darwin called this process "natural selection."

Natural selection accounts for how, after thousands of years, plants and animals can become finely tuned to survive in a specific environment. After a voyage that included his famous visit to the Galápagos Islands, Darwin observed that iguanas had responded to life on different islands there in different ways. He noticed that on some islands they had evolved to eat cactus and on others they had evolved to swim in the ocean and feed on algae. He suspected that natural selection was responsible. Both types of iguanas had most likely evolved from a common ancestor, probably from the rainforests of South or Central America, that had become stranded on the islands thousands of years earlier. Only natural selection could scientifically account for such changes.

Darwin was the first to fully present natural selection as a theory in 1859 in his book *On the Origin of Species*. Like other major theories, such as those of atoms, the solar system, gravity, and the cell, Darwin's theory has been well supported since he presented it. It has been repeatedly confirmed as the best explanation of a broad range of facts and

Although our kinship was clear, this illustration from 1699 shows how poorly the human-ape connection was understood. A baby chimpanzee imported from Africa was mistaken for an adult and is shown walking like a human with a cane.

Flexible shoulders and a keen sense of balance allow this gymnast to stand on one arm with a ball on her head. These characteristics, along with large forward facing eyes, increased brain size, a short snout, fingers that can grasp quickly, fingernails, and long lives, link us to other primates and specifically to apes. We are placed with chimpanzees, gorillas, orangutans, and gibbons in a group called the hominoids.

observations of nature. Though many people of his time believed that humans were created separately from animals—as many people of our time, too, still believe—Darwin argued that we, like all other living things, must have gone through a series of inheritable changes as we evolved. Since apes are our closest animal relatives, Darwin proposed that we must have evolved from apes and that we share a common ancestor with them.

In the late 1880s, convinced that clues to human origins lay in Southeast Asia, a Dutch doctor named Eugène Dubois set off for the islands of Indonesia. There he discovered a skull, a leg bone, and a tooth buried in the banks of the Solo River near Trinil on the island of Java. The creature's brain was about halfway between human and chimpanzee size, but it had features, such as a remarkably humanlike thigh bone, or femur, that showed it was clearly not an ape.

Gibbons are the smallest of living apes.

Gibbons
Genus *Hylobates*

WHAT'S IN A NAME?

Paleoanthropologists classify fossils using a naming system developed by the 18th-century scientist Carolus Linnaeus. When things are classified they are placed into groups and subgroups to clarify relationships. In this system humans are included in the order Primates along with animals such as tarsiers, lemurs, monkeys, and all apes. This is because members of Primates are more similar to each other than they are to other animals, such as bats or whales. There are other, smaller groups within Primates. One is reserved only for apes and humans. It is called the superfamily Hominoidea.

A traditional grouping of apes and humans within Hominoidea places the human lineage alone in the family Hominidae. For many years, members of this family, whether living or extinct, were known as hominids (see below).

Bonobo
Pan paniscus

There are two known species of chimpanzee: chimpanzees and bonobos.

Different family classifications, or groupings, are used by scientists to explain relationships. If one wanted to point to the presence or absence of certain adaptations, such as walking upright on two legs, the traditional grouping at near right works well. If one wanted to stress the close genetic relationship of humans to chimps, as well as the genetic distance between gorillas and orangutans, the grouping at far right can be used.

Genetic research, however, suggests that humans, chimpanzees, and gorillas are genetically closer to each other than any of them are to orangutans or gibbons. Furthermore, chimpanzees and humans are more closely related to each other than either is to gorillas. Scientists are regrouping the apes and humans in Hominoidea to reflect these newly understood genetic distances (see below right). Chimps and gorillas move out of the group they were in with orangutans and into Hominidae with humans. Likewise, chimpanzees move closer to humans and are included in the subfamily Homininae with them. Finally, humans are set apart from chimpanzees in a group that includes only the living and extinct human lineage. The name for this group is the tribe Hominini. Members of this tribe are called hominins. You will see this term used throughout the book.

The names of these groups are arbitrary and, as you can see in the charts below, they do not change the basic relationships of apes and humans. Just the grouping and the names of the groups differ.

Beyond these broad groupings, the naming system of Linnaeus also gives each kind of creature, living or extinct, a name. This is called a **binomial**— or two-part—name; the first is a **genus** name and the second is a **species** name. Modern humans are known as *Homo sapiens*, meaning "wise person."

TRADITIONAL GROUPING

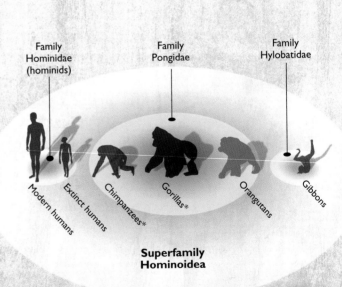

Family Hominidae (hominids)

Family Pongidae

Family Hylobatidae

Modern humans

Extinct humans

Chimpanzees*

Gorillas*

Orangutans

Gibbons

Superfamily Hominoidea

ROBERT HYNES / PORTIA SLOAN

Female (left) and male orangutans
Pongo pygmaeus

Much can be gleaned from binomial names, which are often based on Latin or Greek words carefully chosen by scientists who name fossils. Their names often include the word "pithecus," meaning "ape" in Greek, or the word "ensis," meaning "from." *Australopithecus afarensis*, for example, means "southern ape from the Afar"— a region of Ethiopia where it was found. Just as groupings can differ, scientists can give different genus and species names to the same fossil as a way of communicating their ideas about relationships. One hominin fossil from Africa, for example, has two names: *Homo habilis* and *Homo rudolfensis*. The one used depends on the point being made. To keep things clear, fossils are assigned a specimen number in addition to its binomial name. This way everyone knows what fossil you are talking about no matter what other names are associated with it. The specimen number OH-9, for example, means "Olduvai hominid number nine."

The last common ancestor of orangutans, gorillas, chimpanzees, and humans probably lived over ten million years ago.

Gorillas are close to extinction. Their biggest threat is another ape—humans.

Human
Homo sapiens

GROUPING REFLECTING GENETIC DISTANCE

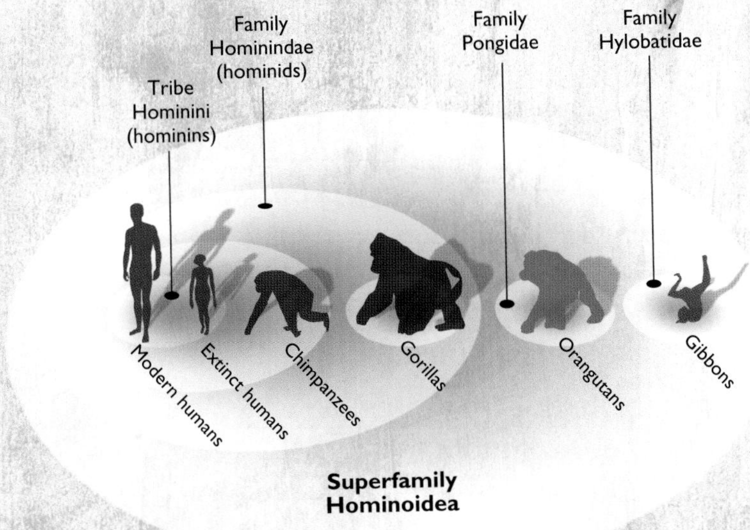

Tribe
Hominini
(hominins)

Family
Hominindae
(hominids)

Family
Pongidae

Family
Hylobatidae

Modern humans

Extinct humans

Chimpanzees

Gorillas

Orangutans

Gibbons

Superfamily Hominoidea

Male (near right) and female gorillas
Gorilla gorilla

* The group that includes hominins and chimpanzees is called Homininae, or hominines, and the group that includes gorillas is called Gorillinae.

Chimpanzees use a wide variety of tools to gain access to food. They use twigs to probe for ants and termites, and stones to smash hard nut shells (above). Our hominin ancestors, such as *Australopithecus africanus* from South Africa (right), may have used tools in these ways also. They probably foraged in trees for nuts and ripe fruit, such as figs, and stayed in groups for safety much as chimpanzees do today.

Using the naming system of Linnaeus, Dubois named his discovery *Pithecanthropus erectus*, meaning "upright apeman." *Pithecanthropus* confirmed in many people's minds that Darwin had been correct about there being a common ancestor of apes and humans in the distant past.

These were the early days of paleoanthropology, the science of studying human ancestors. Since then scientists have unearthed thousands of bones belonging to early humans. In most cases, the original bone material has been replaced by minerals, which makes the bone look and feel like stone. This process, called fossilization, can preserve the shape of bones as fossils for millions of years. In some cases where the preservation is very good, scientists can still see even the most subtle features. Similarities and differences in these features are used to organize our ancestors into groups that show an evolutionary history.

Pithecanthropus was hailed at the time it was found as the most primitive human ancestor, but since then we have learned that it was just one of many different forms of early humans that lived in the last six million years or so. We also know that many of the features and behaviors we associate with being human today evolved in those relatives who lived long ago, even though many of them were quite apelike.

CHAPTER TWO

OUR NEXT OF KIN

All primates walk, run, or climb using four legs as their main way of moving except for one group, the hominins. Millions of years ago an early species of this lineage evolved to stand up straight and walk without waddling. This ability set them apart from all other apes and set them off on an evolutionary experiment all their own.

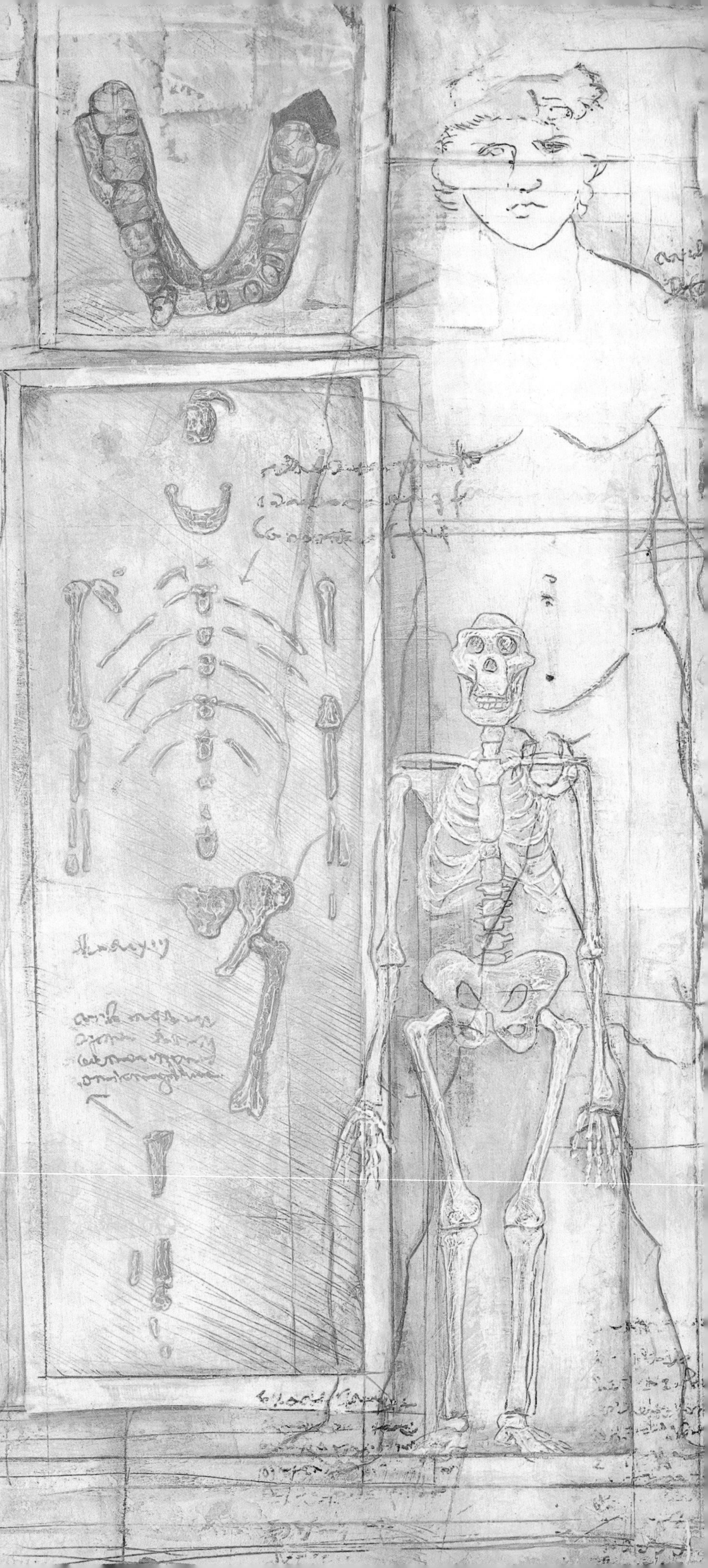

The early hominins, such as *Australopithecus afarensis* (far right), were apes that evolved anatomy that, among other things, made it possible to walk upright. In the background (counter-clockwise from near right) are the fossil remains of the female specimen known as "Lucy," a comparison of Lucy's size to a modern human, a fossil footprint, and the skull and jaw of this hominin.

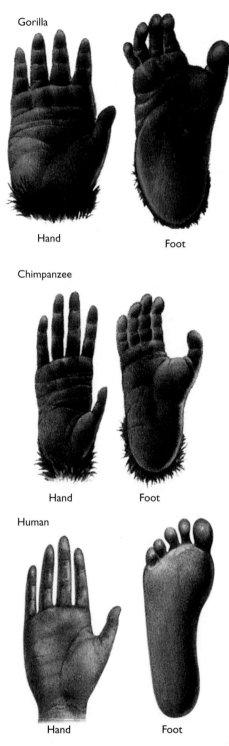

Gorilla

Hand

Foot

Chimpanzee

Hand

Foot

Human

Hand

Foot

The big toes of hominins are not thumblike for grasping as they are in other primates. Some of us can pick up pencils with our toes and some can still climb trees, but we have lost most of the grasping ability in our feet.

Even these earliest hominins had features and behaviors that were clearly humanlike. Walking upright on two legs, or being bipedal, is one of these. Having smaller canine teeth, the ones that are long and sharp in many other apes, is another. Yet the early hominins were quite different from us. Even though we can see something familiar in them, they probably behaved and interacted with their surroundings much as apes do.

When hominins started to split from the other apes is not known precisely. Estimates from DNA and fossils, however, suggest we split from our closest ape relatives, the ancestors we share with chimpanzees, about five to seven million years ago.

Many of the physical requirements for walking upright already existed in primates before our lineage split from other apes. Unlike many mammals with four limbs, primates place their weight on their back legs instead of their front legs when they walk on all fours. This allows them to stand up to reach for branches or walk and jump short distances using their hind limbs. They also have the ability to grasp with their hands and feet. This allows them to move along branches with carefully controlled steps and to hold on with their feet as they stand to reach above them for fruit. This kind of careful walking may have been a good strategy for hunting, since it reduces shaking in branches and frees hands for grabbing prey.

Yet no other animals, not even other primates, walk as we do. When hominins walk we push off with our big toe and swing a leg forward. Our heel hits the ground and the leg straightens under the body, with the knee and lower leg directly under the center of the head. This alignment is important for balance. The hominin thighbone, or femur, is angled inward from the hip to the knee especially to accomplish this balancing act. We think we are walking on two legs, but what is really happening is that we are shifting balance from leg to leg and thus putting all our weight on just one leg at a time. Since our earliest human ancestors, the shape of the whole leg, from hip to toe, gradually evolved to become an important part of efficient hominin movement.

Ape anatomy, on the other hand, has not changed much since our lineages split from each other long ago. Their arms and legs were—and still are—well-suited for a lifestyle that includes climbing. Apes also have kept their thumblike big

While the earliest hominins, such as *Australopithecus afarensis* (center), had a chimp-size body, there are important differences. Its hip, or pelvis, for example, is bowl-shaped like a modern human. Its femur is angled in toward the center of the body in a similar way as well. Both of these features are related to maintaining balance over two feet. The small brain and the relatively long arms of *Australopithecus afarensis*, however, are more like a chimpanzee.

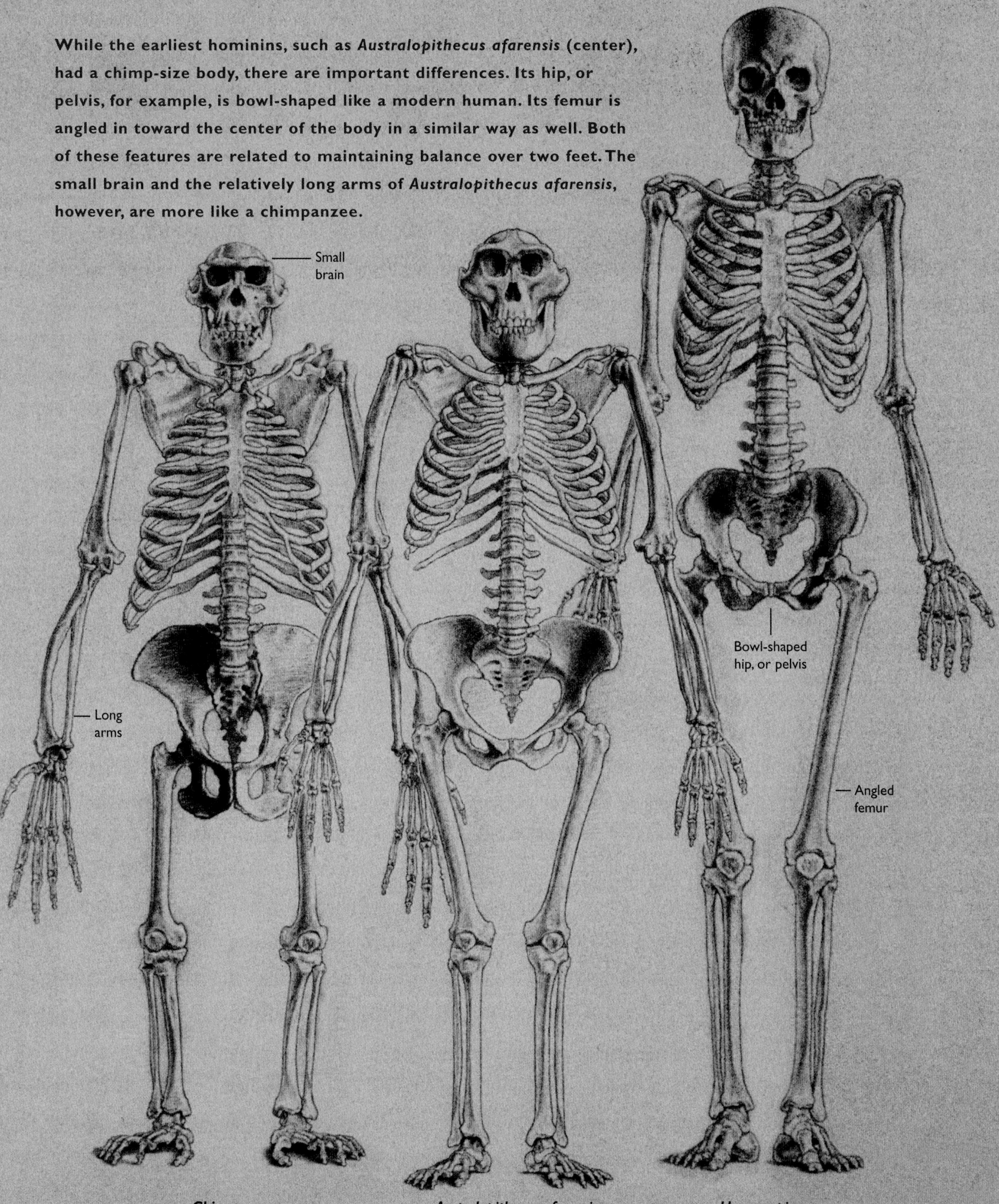

Small brain

Long arms

Bowl-shaped hip, or pelvis

Angled femur

Chimpanzee
(male)

Australopithecus afarensis
(male)

Homo sapiens
(male)

Chimpanzees walk on all fours (above), unlike hominins such as *Australopithecus afarensis* (reconstructed, far right), which walked on two legs. A comparison of spines (center) shows part of the reason why. The chimp spine (far right shadow) is arched and attaches near the back of the skull. This makes a chimp hunch over. The spine of *Australopithecus afarensis* (near right), on the other hand, is not arched and attaches to the center of the skull, just like a modern human spine and skull (center shadow).

toes, which, being separate from the other toes, are great for grasping branches and even food, but they are not great for bipedal walking.

Upright walking and running is not as fast or as graceful as walking on all fours can be, but the system worked well enough for our ancestors to have survived. It worked so well that our legs are only slightly different from those of hominins that lived millions of years ago. But being an effective bipedal creature involved other changes beyond our lower limbs.

The parts of the hominin body that underwent big changes as we became bipedal are our spines, skulls, and our hips, or pelvises. Partly for balance, but also to enable us to look forward as we walk upright, our spine had to evolve from being a C-shaped arch to an S-shape. As part of this change, the hole in the base of our skull that allows the spinal cord to connect to the brain shifted forward. This allows our head to be balanced perfectly over our spine. The large flat blades of bone that form our pelvis changed from being long, flat, and positioned near the back to being more sturdy, shorter, bowl-shaped, and oriented to the sides of our body. This helps support and balance the upper body and repositioned muscles for bipedal walking.

Many fossil bones of early humans who lived in Africa around three to four million years

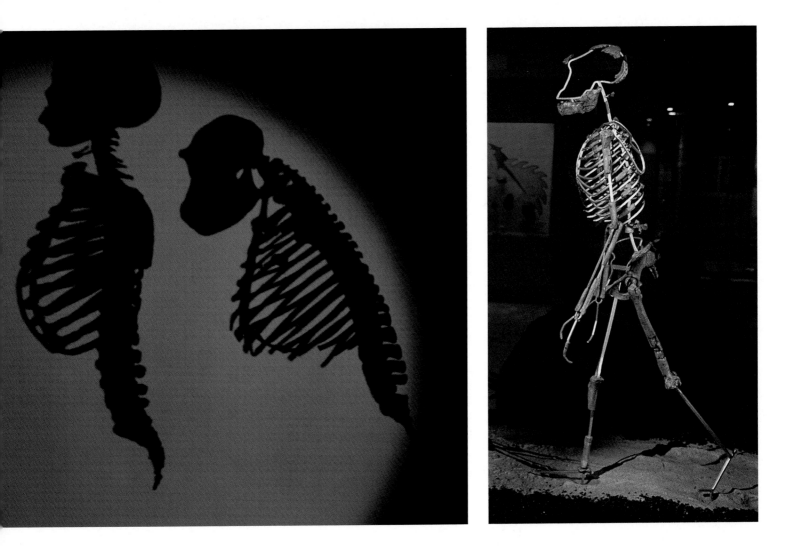

ago, such as *Australopithecus anamensis, Australopithecus afarensis*, and *Australopithecus africanus* show that they were bipedal. We can see this in the shape of pelvises, legs, feet, spines, and skulls that have been preserved.

Another remarkable line of evidence comes from Laetoli in Tanzania. There, in 1976, scientists found a path of 54 footprints *(see page 4)*. The footprints show that at least two creatures with feet shaped like modern humans had walked there much like we do. The footprints were preserved in volcanic ash, one of the most useful materials for determining the age of geological layers and the fossils associated with them. Dating of the volcanic ash shows that the footprints were made between 3.6 and 3.8 million years ago. There were two creatures living at the time that could have made these footprints: *Kenyanthropus platyops* and *Australopithecus afarensis*. *Australopithecus afarensis* is the leading suspect because its fossilized bones have also been found at Laetoli *(see map on page 40 for location of fossil sites)*.

Australopithecus afarensis was about the same size—both in brain and brawn—as an adult chimpanzee. It is best known from well-preserved fossils found farther north, in Ethiopia. There, in 1974, scientists unearthed a specimen about three million years old that for decades was the earliest known and most complete fossil human skeleton. Its nickname is "Lucy."

Scientists can figure out what kinds of environments early hominins lived in by studying plant and animal fossils as well as the geology of an area where bones are found. Fossils of *Australopithecus afarensis* are found in the driest parts of Ethiopia near sea level. When these hominins lived there more than three million years ago, the area was much higher in elevation.

There was lots of water, as well as lush forests like the one shown above. Saying how hominins behaved in these environments is more difficult. Most scientists agree that they would probably remind us of apes living today. The anatomical differences between hominins and other apes, however, would eventually lead to very different lifestyles.

25

Fossils of even older specimens, however, hint strongly that bipedalism evolved earlier. The fragmentary leg bones of *Orrorin tugenensis* from the Tugen Hills of Kenya are dated at six million years old. There is enough fossil bone to see that the legs were angled toward the center of the body like a hominin's. An even older specimen, *Sahelanthropus tchadensis* from Chad, is reported to be between six and seven million years old. Its large brow and small canine teeth are similar to what scientists expect to see in hominins, but it had an ape-size brain.

Since the time of the earliest hominins, our brains have increased almost four times in volume. This certainly brought advantages such as improved muscle control and perception. It also brought problems: Bigger-brained infants required a wider birth canal in the mother's pelvis to pass through. Wider birth canals meant wider female pelvises, however, and that threatened to throw off the balancing act that efficient walking required.

Despite this, female pelvises in hominins did become wider over time, and athletic records today show the result: modern human females

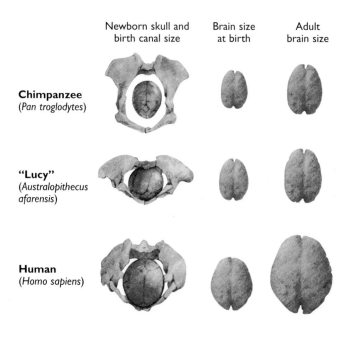

Newborn skull and birth canal size — Brain size at birth — Adult brain size

Chimpanzee (*Pan troglodytes*)

"Lucy" (*Australopithecus afarensis*)

Human (*Homo sapiens*)

The use of stone tools made fat-rich bone marrow and brains a regular part of the diet of hominins such as *Homo habilis* (opposite). These new food sources were important for brain growth. The chart above compares the brains and the skulls and pelvises in birth position of a chimpanzee, the australopithecine "Lucy," and a modern human. Most human brain growth occurs after birth, which is one reason why newborn humans remain helpless longer than chimp babies.

are slightly slower than males. But how then did our ancestors bear bigger-brained babies without becoming too slow at moving to avoid predators? How could brains continue to get bigger without an ever-widening birth canal in the pelvis? The solution that evolved among hominins was that babies were born at a less developed stage, that is, before their brains became too large for the birth canal. As a result, human babies are born less developed, and stay helpless longer, than the babies of great apes. Human babies are unable to see well, unable to get around, and unable to feed themselves for a long time after birth.

Giving birth to big-brained, helpless infants must have had a huge impact on hominin life. Because of their head size, hominins were probably difficult to give birth to compared to ape babies. And once born, they probably required a greater investment of time and energy from their mothers. Hominin mothers needed to eat more foods, such as bone marrow and animal brains, that provided high concentrations of dietary fats. This was so they could provide the fattier nutrient-rich milk their infants needed to fuel their brain growth. Unlike other apes, whose babies cling to them with hands and feet, hominin mothers had to carry their babies in their arms. It is difficult to get anything done while carrying a baby in your arms.

This greater investment in offspring probably affected whole hominin social groups, not just mothers. Scientists who study living apes and human hunter-gatherer societies feel there is much we can learn from them about the possible origins of hominin social behavior. They suggest that early hominins may have had to gather more food than they needed as individuals in order to supply mothers with extra food during nursing or to help feed the young, just as hunter-gatherer groups do today. Close relatives may have helped females give birth and chipped in by baby-sitting. These relatives might even have adopted an infant if a mother died, as happens among apes today. The social bonds that grew as a result of all these behaviors, particularly among females, could have increased the chances of survival for infants. It could also have improved the ability of mothers to have more offspring in their fertile years. This could have been a major advantage for the survival of a group.

WILLIAM KIMBEL ◄

MICHAEL NICHOLS ▶

Hominins have smaller canine teeth, shorter snouts, and larger molars than other apes. These differences are apparent in these views that compare, from left to right, a set of chimpanzee teeth to an australopithecine and a modern human.

What about the males? Hominin males were larger than females, but the size differences between males and females became smaller over time so that today there is less difference between the sexes among humans than there is in orangutans, gorillas, or chimpanzees. It is possible that the difference in body size between the hominin sexes decreased because hominin society was structured in a way where size and other physical differences were not very important for survival.

The canine teeth, used by male apes to scare off rivals or intruders, are another sexual difference in primates. In great apes the canines are larger in males than in females, and this was also true for the early hominins. But as time went on, the canines of males shrank to the point where there was little difference between the sexes. Some scientists have suggested that fighting between males may have been a disadvantage in a group where cooperation and support were needed to survive. Perhaps the males who were best at supporting the needs of the group through food gathering were more sought after as mates than the ones with long sharp teeth.

Food gathering was especially important to hominins because their growing brains were energy hogs. Human brains today are only two percent of the body in weight, but at rest they require 20 to 25 percent of the energy the body produces. This compares to 8 to 10 percent in nonhuman primates. This means that as brains grew, the hominin diet needed to include foods

Many chimpanzee groups are active and effective hunters. Hunting is often a collaborative effort, with males working as a team to corner prey, such as monkeys. It is possible that early hominins hunted as well, but we cannot be sure if they captured their own prey or scavenged the kills of other animals, or both.

that were as high in energy-yielding nutrition as possible. Fruits and nuts are good for this, but these do not compare to meat.

There is no fossil evidence that hominins that lived much before 2.5 million years ago ate meat. That date marks when the earliest known stone tools suitable for slicing meat and smashing bone appear in the fossil record. There is no reason, however, to rule out meat-eating before tools. Some of the earliest known hominins, such as *Ardipithecus ramidus*, lived 5.8 million years ago in environments that were not too different from those in which some modern chimpanzees hunt. Among the remains of *Ardipithecus* scientists found the fossil bones of colobus monkeys and small antelopes, favorite foods of today's chimpanzees. If early hominins such as *Ardipithecus* did not hunt, it was probably not for lack of prey.

If such early hominins did not hunt, another source of meat was the carcasses of animals killed by others. Chimpanzees do not scavenge, but it is possible that our ancestors did. There were enough carcasses present in the environments our ancestors lived in to provide many opportunities to obtain meat. To eat the meat of carcasses, however, an animal needs sharp teeth and claws—two things hominins did not possess.

HOW OLD IS IT?

The age of a fossil is one of the most important things for a paleoanthropologist to figure out. This is because a key part of understanding our evolutionary history is knowing when changes occurred. Luckily, there are lots of clues at a dig site that can help scientists discover how old the site and its fossils are. To be as accurate as possible, scientists use several methods to establish a date rather than just one. Here are a few of them.

Stratigraphic dating is based on studying the layers of earth and rock at a fossil site. These layers—called strata—were formed as earth, rock, and vegetation were deposited, one on top of the other, over long periods of time. You can see strata clearly in many road cuts along highways where the layers of earth or rock have different colors and textures. Each layer represents what that place was like at a particular time. A site may have been under water at one time and dried out as a desert at another. Each of these

Paranthropus boisei
1.7 million years old
Lake Turkana, Kenya
fossil name: KNM-ER 406

conditions leaves a different kind of deposit.

In general, older strata lie below younger ones. If a fossil is found in a lower layer, then it is likely to be older than fossils found in a higher layer. By comparing the order of layers found at a site to the order known from other locations, geologists can

often figure out what time period a layer is from.

Faunal dating works in a somewhat similar way, but it relies on what scientists know about the order in which extinct forms of animal life, or fauna, appeared. The fossil remains of elephants, pigs, antelopes, and even mouse-like creatures called voles are often found along with fossils of human ancestors. The evolutionary history of these animals is so well known that their presence can be used to estimate age. If human remains are found with an earlier form of pig, for instance, it suggests an older age than if they were found with a more recent type of pig.

Stratigraphic and faunal dating are known as **relative dating** methods because they provide information about the order of events relative to each

Stone tools
1.8 to 1.7 million years old
Dmanisi, Georgia

Absolute Dating Methods

Years ago*

Present	100,000	200,000	300,000	400,000	500,000	600,000	700,000

U

Potassium to argon (used on minerals)

Electron spin resonance (used on minerals, tooth enamel, shell, coral)

Thermoluminescence (used on minerals, natural glass) 0 to 500,000 years

Carbon 14 (used on shell, wood, bone, teeth) 0 to 50,000 years

*At this scale the 4.6 billion year mark would be about fourteen football fields away

other and thus can provide an age range, but they cannot establish a precise date. That is where *absolute dating* comes in.

Absolute dating methods focus on elements that are either closely associated with, or actually part of, human fossils. One type of absolute dating, called *radio-metric dating*, is based on the fact that certain elements, such as potassium and carbon, change from one form to another at known rates. This process is called radioactive decay.

Two radiometric dating methods commonly used to estimate the age of fossil human ancestor sites are potassium-argon and carbon dating. *Potassium-argon dating* can be used to date material within a time range of about 10,000 to 3 billion years. It is best at dating older material, however. *Carbon dating* is very useful for dating

material that is less than 40,000 years old, but it can be stretched to 50,000 years. One of the best sources of potassium for dating comes from the ash of volcanic eruptions or from volcanic rock. Organic material, such as shell, wood, bone, and teeth, is useful for carbon dating. Carbon dating is frequently used to date charcoal from hearths or plant material, such as grain or cloth fibers.

Other dating methods vary widely. Using *thermolumines-cence* and *electron spin resonance* scientists measure time by observing how exposure to heat or light has affected material found near a specimen. These methods have been used successfully on fossilized teeth, flint, limestone, coral, and even egg shells.

Geomagnetic polarity reversals

Clay statuette
34,000 to 26,500 years old
Dolní Věstonice, Czech Republic

Sabretooth cat
1.8 to 1.7 million years old
Dmanisi, Georgia

create a record of ancient flip-flops in the magnetic north and south poles of the Earth. These can be used to date fossil sites, too, if strata containing evidence of magnetic switches are found nearby.

Using dating methods such as these, scientists have estimated that the Earth is 4.6 billion years old and that life on Earth is 3.8 billion years old. To get an idea of how recently humans evolved, imagine that those 4.6 billion years are just one day. During this day, which began just after midnight, life on Earth appeared at about 4:00 a.m. Dinosaurs roamed about 11:00 p.m. The first hominins appeared about two minutes to midnight. Modern humans showed up about two or three seconds before the clock struck twelve.

800,000   900,000   1,000,000

lead (used on minerals) 1 million to 4.6 billion years *

10,000 to 3 billion years

1,000 to 1 million years

Volcanic rock from the Afar region of Ethiopia

There are many types of absolute dating methods, some of which are shown at left. Each is useful for finding the age of things within a certain time range. These time ranges are based on the rate of radioactive decay of the element in the sample being dated.

The potassium-argon method, for example, measures the potassium and argon found in volcanic rock. As radioactive potassium decays, it turns into argon. The greater the proportion of argon in a sample, the older it is because there has been more time for the potassium to change. The greater the proportion of potassium, the younger it is.

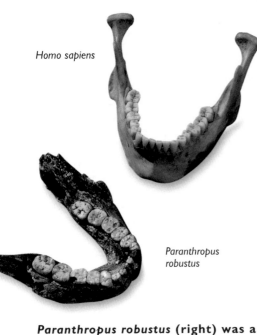

Homo sapiens

Paranthropus
robustus

Paranthropus robustus (right) was a member of a lineage of hominins that evolved huge molars (above, compared to modern human) and jaw muscles suitable for crushing plant material. Two million years ago, *Paranthropus* and a member of our own genus, *Homo*, roamed southern Africa. An encounter between them, such as the one hinted at by a shadow in the painting at right, was entirely possible.

Making and using simple stone tools does not necessarily require a big brain or a human-like hand. Chimpanzees, for example, use stones as hammers and anvils, as well as for chopping. Hominins probably used tools this way, too. But they were also doing something unlike anything a wild chimpanzee does. They were making cutting tools.

Cutting tools make up for the fact that we do not have the natural meat-processing equipment of sharp teeth and claws that other predators have. These tools are sharp-edged stones chipped off another rock, often a large pebble, called a core. A core could be used over and over to make many sharp flakes. The two-and-a-half million-year-old cutting tools found at Gona in the Afar region of Ethiopia were little more than stones that had been broken this way to produce sharp edges. But they were sharp enough to cut flesh. Other stones found there were large enough to shatter bone.

Australopithecus garhi, an early hominin fossil also from Ethiopia, could have been an early cutting-tool maker. It lived between two and three million years ago, and its fossils were found near the remains of animals whose bones had been broken and cut by stone tools. If it was the tool maker, this hominin was using its brain and hands in a very different way from chimps.

Over time, the brain size of hominins increased, and their hands became specialized for gripping small things precisely with the thumb and fingers. They could use sharp tools and eat small foods such as nuts and berries. Both hand and brain were crucial to later hominins' ability to make more complex tools.

Around the same time that tools were starting to appear, a different kind of hominin with huge jaws packed with big molar teeth emerged. When they were first discovered, members of this group were sometimes called "Nutcracker Man" because unlike other hominins, their teeth and jaws muscles had evolved into what must have been a very strong machine for crunching and grinding food. These hominins are placed in a genus called *Paranthropus* or they may be placed in the genus *Australopithecus*. Their lineage did not survive past one million years ago. Why?

Scientists once thought the paranthropines became extinct because the capacity to use tools never evolved in their lineage or because they depended too much on a particular food, such as large seeds. If this were true and their food source disappeared, they might not have been flexible enough to adapt to new conditions. This view, however, is changing. There is now evidence that paranthropines' diet was not unlike that of other hominins. It included termites, the root bulbs of plants, and perhaps even meat. Tools have also been found near the bones of paranthropines such as *Paranthropus robustus,* which lived two million years ago in South Africa. Among these are bone tools that show the type of wear one would expect from digging. These are the earliest known bone tools. So why did the paranthropines go extinct? We do not know.

Not just the paranthropines, but all of our bipedal ancestors experienced the same evolutionary forces that have driven other creatures to extinction. *Sahelanthropus, Orrorin, Ardipithecus, Australopithecus,* and *Kenyanthropus* all vanished. Why so many died off we may never know, but in evolution extinction is common. It is possible that some of the later hominins, such as the paranthropines, were driven into extinction through competition with other hominin groups alive at the time. Whatever the case, by one million years ago *Homo,* our group, was the only genus left.

THE EARLY HOMININS

Africa was thought by some scientists to be a good place to find early human fossils since it was where our close relatives, chimpanzees and gorillas, lived. Yet it was not until the 1920s that a hominin fossil was found there.

The first early hominin fossils found in Africa were from South Africa. The name "*Australopithecus*," in fact, means "Southern ape." The name was first given to a remarkably preserved baby hominin skull

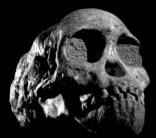

Australopithecus africanus
2.3 million years old, South Africa
fossil name: TAUNG CHILD

known as the Taung Child (above).

Since then, Africa has been the source of many early hominin discoveries. One reason is that the eastern side of the continent of Africa has been ripped open and uplifted in a geological phenomenon known as the Rift Valley. Fossil-rich sediments that are millions of years old are exposed in many places along this rift (see page 40).

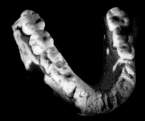

Australopithecus afarensis
3.6 million years old, Tanzania
fossil name: L.H.-4

In 1959 a fossil skull was discovered at Olduvai Gorge in the Rift Valley in what is now Tanzania. That fossil, *Zinjanthropus boisei*, was celebrated as an early human relative at the time, but it has since been redated, renamed (it is now *Paranthropus boisei*), and taken out of the direct ancestry of modern humans. There has been no shortage of other fossils discovered in East Africa since then, however, to put into the human family tree.

Far to the north of Olduvai Gorge, but along the same rift valley system, lies an area in the Afar region of Ethiopia called Hadar. It was here that the 3.2-million-year-old skeleton known as "Lucy" was found in 1974 (see

Ardipithecus ramidus (piece of jaw with tooth)
4.4 million years old, Ethiopia
fossil name: ARA-VP-1/129

National Museum of Ethiopia, Addis Ababa
© 1994 Tim D. White/Brill Atlanta

photo page 22). "Lucy" was classified as *Australopithecus afarensis*, the same species scientists suspect of making the footprints at Laetoli in Tanzania (left and page 4).

Just south of Hadar in an area called the Middle Awash, scientists discovered some very early hominins in a geological sequence that stretches back continuously for six million years. The oldest bones there belong to the species *Ardipithecus ramidus*, which lived in that area for over one million years.

Fossils of hominins from many different times have also been found around Lake Turkana, which lies farther south along the rift in

Australopithecus anamensis
4.1 million years old, Kenya
fossil name: KNM-KP 29285

Kenya. Among the many hominins found there, scientists discovered one that is now the earliest and most primitive known australopithecine. It was named *Australopithecus anamensis*. Its partial lower leg bone, or tibia (above), shows that it was bipedal. Other early hominins found in this area include *Kenyanthropus platyops* (see page 5) and the earliest known member

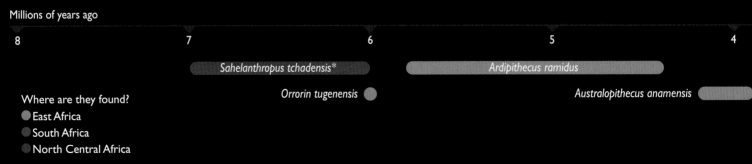

Millions of years ago

| 8 | 7 | 6 | 5 | 4 |

*Sahelanthropus tchadensis**

Ardipithecus ramidus

Where are they found?
- East Africa
- South Africa
- North Central Africa

Orrorin tugenensis

Australopithecus anamensis

*These hominins are known only from a single specimen and only an age range is available.

Homo habilis
or *Australopithecus habilis*
1.9 million years old, Kenya
fossil name: KMN-ER 1813

of our own genus, *Homo habilis.*
   The oldest known hominin was not found in the Rift Valley or South Africa. *Sahelanthropus tchadensis*, a six to seven million-year-old hominin, was discovered at Toros-Menalla in Chad. This is over 1,500 miles west of other hominin fossil sites in the Rift Valley. This and another hominin found in Chad in the 1990s, *Australopithecus bahrelghazali*, suggests that hominins were widespread in Africa millions of years ago.

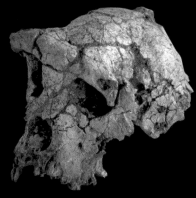

Sahelanthropus tchadensis
6 to 7 million years old, Chad
fossil name: TM 266-01-060-1

Copyright © Mission Paléoanthropologique
Franco-Tchadienne

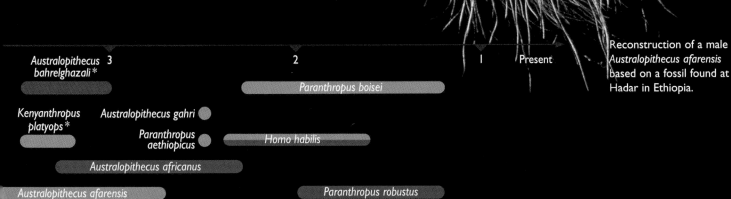

Reconstruction of a male
Australopithecus afarensis
based on a fossil found at
Hadar in Ethiopia.

JOHN GURCHE ▲

Australopithecus bahrelghazali *	3		2		1	Present
Kenyanthropus platyops *		*Australopithecus gahri* ●		*Paranthropus boisei*		
		Paranthropus aethiopicus ●		*Homo habilis*		
		Australopithecus africanus				
Australopithecus afarensis				*Paranthropus robustus*		

35

CHAPTER THREE

OUT OF AFRICA

For millions of years after their origin, hominins remained in Africa. When they roamed off the continent around 1.8 million years ago, they left evidence of their existence at places in Europe and Asia that were separated by thousands of miles. What the human ancestor that left Africa was like and what caused it to expand its range is a subject of much debate.

Did big brains and big bodies enable these early humans to roam farther than before? Or was it a different kind of tool that allowed them to access new food sources in new territory? Perhaps it was climate change that allowed them to expand their range by creating new connections between continents. Newly discovered fossils and genetic evidence are providing scientists with the clues that may lead to some answers.

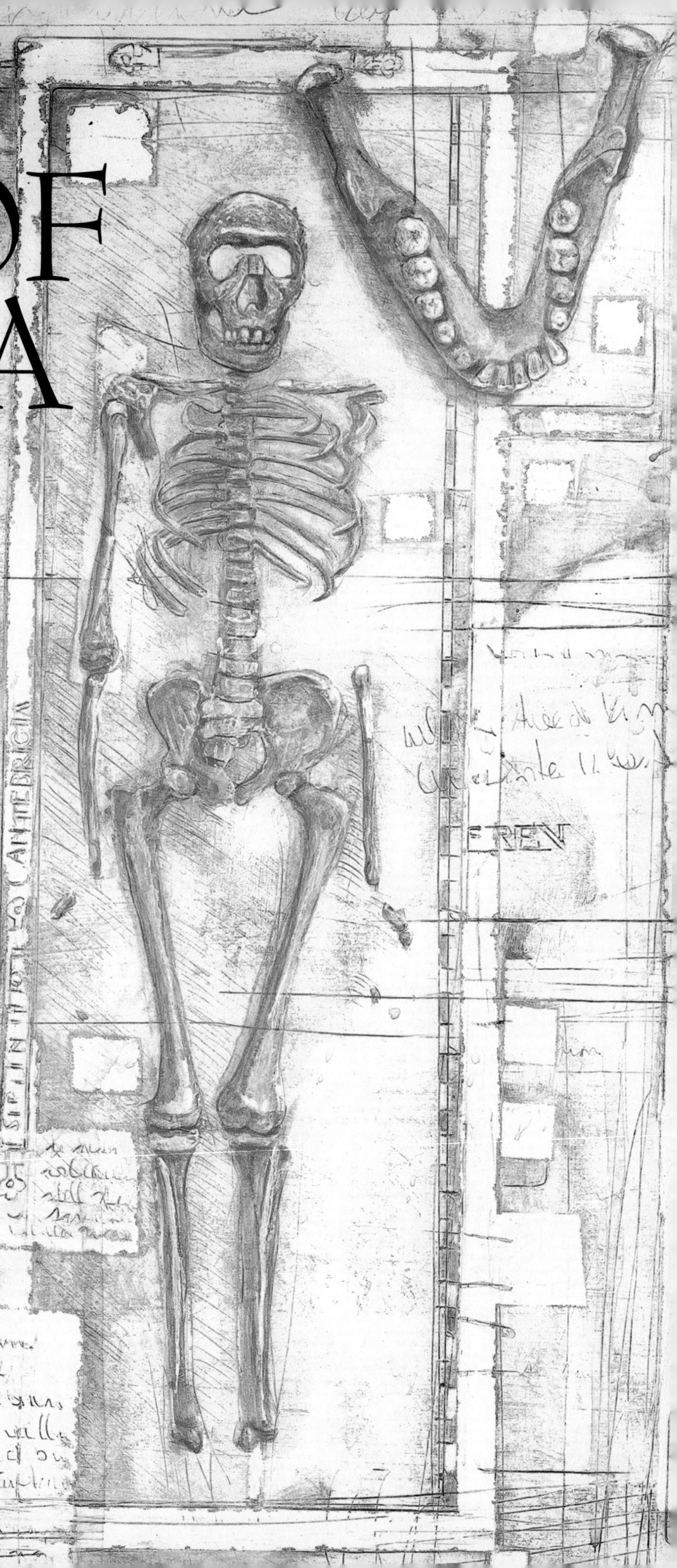

Homo erectus, **represented here by the Nariokotome boy (far right, boy and skull), had a skeleton (near right, skeleton and jaw) much like a modern human's, but a small brain. This species is credited with introducing a new kind of stone tool, the hand axe (bottom right).**

NABIOKOTOM

KNM-WT

Homo erectus
from Dmanisi

GOURAM TSIBAKHASHVILI Courtesy of DAVID LORDKIPANIDZE

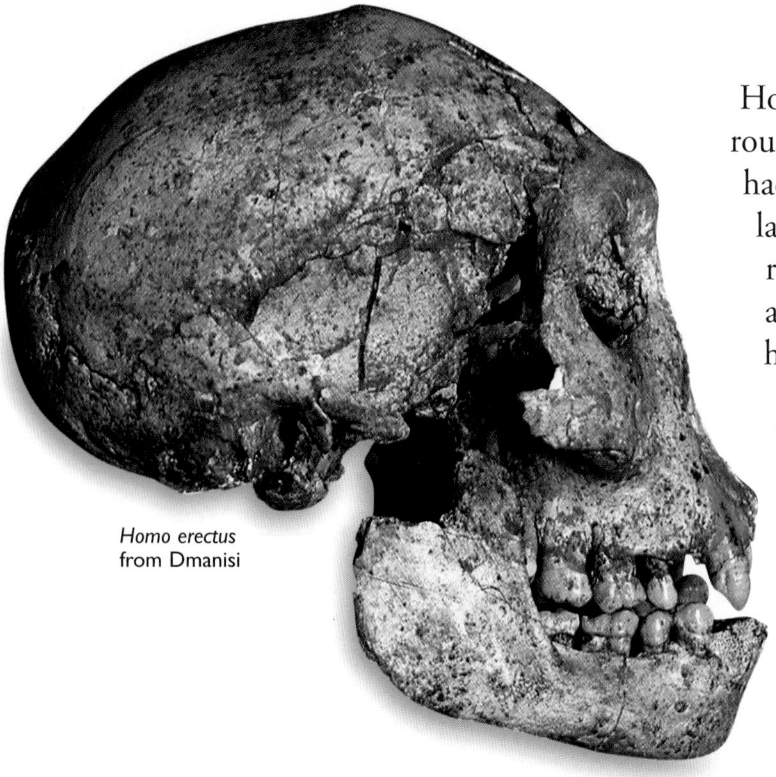

Hominins from this important time interval, roughly two million years to 500,000 years ago, had much larger brains than apes and bodies as large as modern humans. They are probably responsible for starting to make the hand axe—a very different type of tool than any other hominins made before them.

Did this make them modern humans? No. These hominins, known as *Homo erectus*, had brains that were still small compared to those of humans today. It is unlikely that they could speak and, from what we know, they showed no signs of abstract thinking or symbolic behavior. While they certainly showed signs of innovation with the hand axe and other tools, these hominins stuck more or less with that same plan for a million years. That is *much* less innovation than we would expect to see in modern humans.

Homo erectus did, however, show signs of early complex behavior, as did its predecessor, *Homo habilis*. The tools and remains of meals these hominins left behind show paleoanthropologists that over time they developed a deeper understanding of their environments. For example, they not only knew where to find food, but they brought stones from far away to process the meat when they found it. This kind of mastery of their habitat was probably important to their success at expanding their range. Eventually they expanded right out of Africa.

The earliest evidence of hominins outside Africa comes from two places. One is far north of Africa at a site called Dmanisi in the Eurasian country of Georgia, and the other is on the island of Java in Indonesia about 5,000 miles to the east. The distance between

A small skull found at Dmanisi in Georgia (above) hints that adult *Homo erectus* may have ranged in size from six feet tall down to the size of *Homo habilis*- about four feet.

When *Homo erectus* left Africa, it may have been expanding its range in response to climate change. Other warm weather creatures, such as sabre-tooth cats, hyenas, early giraffes, and giant ostriches (opposite) did the same.

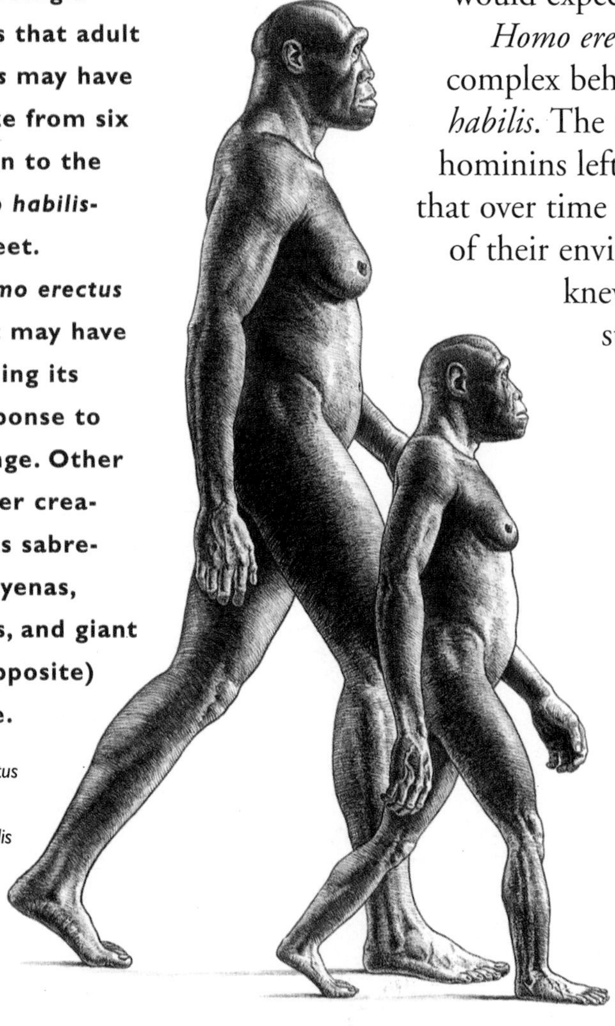

Female *Homo erectus*
5 ft 3 in 117 lbs

Female *Homo habilis*
3 ft 10 in 71 lbs

JOHN GURCHE

these two sites is similar to the distance between New York and Hawaii *(see page 40)*. Dmanisi is much closer to Africa than Java is. It lies in rugged terrain on the eastern shore of the Black Sea. There, archaeologists were digging on a hilltop site in the middle of the ruins of a medieval village when they found animal bones. A zoologist recognized that these were not the remains of garbage from a medieval feast but the bones of animals that died between 1.8 and 1.7 million years ago. Further digging discovered more animals, including rhinoceroses, ostriches, and giraffes—and the remains of *Homo erectus.*

Around the time that *Homo erectus* lived at Dmanisi, Earth's climate was alternating between being warm and wet and cool and dry. During warm and wet times, forests would extend beyond the range they occupied during cool, dry periods. When it was cool and dry, sea levels would drop as water was locked up in sea ice and glaciers. Both of these situations created pathways that might have allowed hominins and other animals to expand north through what are now very dry areas in northeast Africa and the Middle East. At some point the level of the Red Sea might have been low enough for hominins to cross what might then have been only two or three miles of water separating Africa from Asia between Djibouti and Yemen. Such pathways must have extended not only north to Dmanisi, but all the way to Java in the east. When sea levels were low, even Java, which is now an island, could have been reached on foot. Dating of fossils from Java indicates they might be as old as Dmanisi, but this is controversial. If it is true, however, *Homo erectus* may have arrived in Java at more or less the same time as it did at Dmanisi. Many scientists wonder what it was about *Homo erectus* that made it, and not earlier hominins in Africa, the one to expand beyond the African cradle.

Oldowan chopper and flakes
2.5 million years old

Early Acheulean hand axe
1.5 million years old

Acheulean hand axe
1 million years old

St. Acheul, France
Hand axe
300,000 years old

London, United Kingdom
Boxgrove
Schöningen
Berlin, Germany
Bilzingsleben
St. Acheul
Mauer, Heidelberg
Paris, France

EUROPE
Eurasia

Caspian Sea
Black Sea

Atapuerca (Gran Dolina, La Sima de los Huesos)
Terra Amata
Arago
Rome, Italy
Ceprano
Dmanisi
Tbilisi, Georgia
Torralba, Ambrona
Madrid, Spain
Venta Micena
Petralona
Athens, Greece

Mediterranean Sea

Gesher Benot Ya'acov
Jerusalem, Israel
Ubeidiya

Middle East

AFRICA

Red Sea

Toros-Menalla
Bahr el Ghazal
N'Djamena, Chad

Sanaa, Yemen
Djibouti, Djibouti
Hadar, Aramis, Gona
Afar region
Addis Ababa, Ethiopia
Konso-Gardula
Omo
Nariokotome
Lake Turkana
Kanapoi
Tugen Hills
Olorgesailie
Nairobi, Kenya
Olduvai Gorge
Laetoli
Dodoma, Tanzania
Rift Valley fossil sites
Dar es Salaam, Tanzania

KEY

● Fossil sites

• *Capitals of countries with fossil sites shown on this map*

Tools are shown approximately to scale

Kabwe (Broken Hill)
Lusaka, Zambia

Pretoria, South Africa
Taung
Swartkrans
Bloemfontein, South Africa

Cape Town, South Africa

TRAIL OF TOOLS

Hominins left a trail of tools that allows us to trace both their technological advances and their expansion out of their African cradle. The earliest known tools are from Gona in Ethiopia, where stone flakes and pebbles with sharp edges, called choppers, are the first evidence that hominins were using tools to get meat. At Dmanisi, Georgia, one of the earliest known sites outside Africa, many of the tools left by our ancestors are similar to those found at Gona. These tools represent the Oldowan tool industry, named after a simple tool-making style identified in the oldest hominin layers at Olduvai Gorge in Tanzania.

At more recent sites, such as Ubeidiya in Israel, and the younger strata at Olduvai Gorge, hominins, probably *Homo erectus*, were making crude hand axes. These were larger than Oldowan tools and had points suitable for digging, chopping, or cutting. With time, our ancestors perfected this technology and were making finely crafted hand axes, such as those found at Olorgesailie in Kenya, and at European sites such as St. Acheul in France, Boxgrove in the United Kingdom, and Venta Micena in Spain. These hand axes are part of what is known as the Acheulean tool industry, which lasted for over a million years.

Olorgesailie, Kenya
Hand axe
780,000 years old

Gona, Ethiopia
Chopper
2.5 million years old

Olduvai Gorge, Tanzania
Hand axe
1.5 million years old

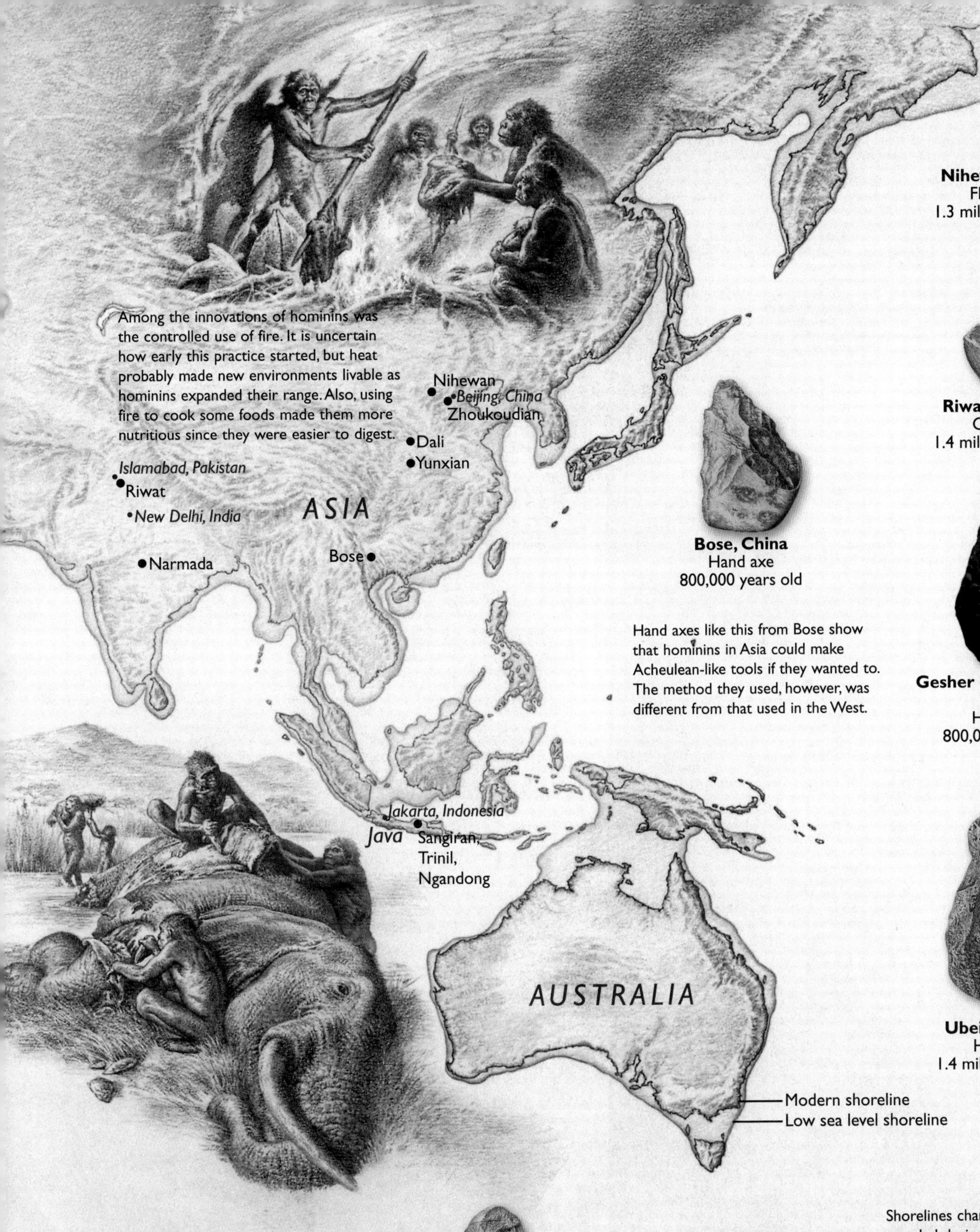

Among the innovations of hominins was the controlled use of fire. It is uncertain how early this practice started, but heat probably made new environments livable as hominins expanded their range. Also, using fire to cook some foods made them more nutritious since they were easier to digest.

Nihewan, China
Flake tool
1.3 million years old

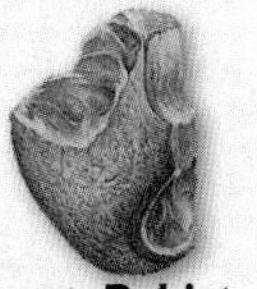

Riwat, Pakistan
Chopper
1.4 million years old

Nihewan
•*Beijing, China*
Zhoukoudian

•Dali
•Yunxian

Islamabad, Pakistan
•Riwat

•*New Delhi, India*

ASIA

•Narmada

Bose •

Bose, China
Hand axe
800,000 years old

Hand axes like this from Bose show that hominins in Asia could make Acheulean-like tools if they wanted to. The method they used, however, was different from that used in the West.

Gesher Benot Ya'acov, Israel
Hand axe
800,000 years old

Jakarta, Indonesia
Java Sangiran,
Trinil,
Ngandong

AUSTRALIA

Ubeidiya, Israel
Hand axe
1.4 million years old

—— Modern shoreline
—— Low sea level shoreline

At Olorgesailie, sharp flakes were detached from hand axes and used to cut into the flesh of an elephant. This technology probably helped *Homo erectus* and later hominins include large quantities of meat in their diet.

Gran Dolina, Spain
Chopper
800,000 years old

Dmanisi, Georgia
Flake tool
1.8-1.7 million years old

Shorelines changed as the sea receded during times when the climate was drier and cooler than today. This happened periodically during the time of *Homo erectus*. It is easy to see how climate change can affect pathways between regions.

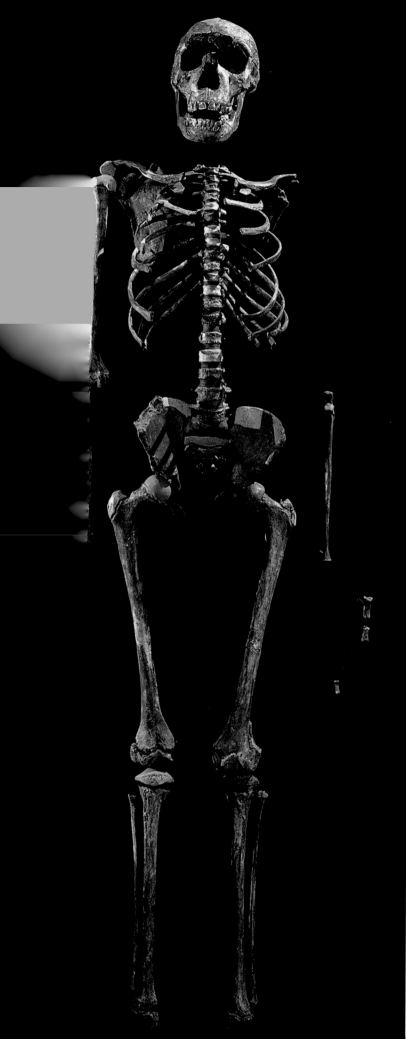

Almost every *Homo erectus* specimen found prior to 2001, whether it was from Java, Africa, or elsewhere, showed that *Homo erectus* was a relatively large hominin. Seeing this, scientists suggested that perhaps one reason *Homo erectus* was able to leave Africa was because it had body proportions much like modern humans and a brain larger than any hominin before.

According to this view, a very good model for what the first humans out of Africa would have been like is the almost complete skeleton of a young male found at Nariokotome in Kenya. He was quite similar to modern humans in body proportion, but he was quite tall for his age by modern human standards. He may have been only seven years old, but he was 5 feet 3 inches tall and probably nearing his adult height. This growth pattern is more similar to apes than to modern humans. His brain, while bigger than that of earlier hominins, was the size of a one-year-old child's today.

This view that the earliest hominins to leave Africa had to be large like the Nariokotome boy, however, is changing. One of the hominins found at Dmanisi suggests that *Homo erectus* included both large and small individuals. They may have been varied in size just like modern humans. Perhaps bodies and brains did not have to be as large as we once thought for hominins to manage the expansion out of Africa.

Homo erectus was probably the first

The Nariokotome boy was discovered at a site of that name in Kenya in 1984. In most proportions he was like a modern human, but his bones were thicker, and he probably could not speak. His teeth and jaws show that he had a bad tooth infection.

hominin to use stone tools bigger than a fist, but the earliest *Homo erectus* in Africa, also known as *Homo ergaster*, used small Oldowan-style ones. Prior to the discoveries at Dmanisi, some scientists suggested that the changes in behavior connected to using large tools—particularly hunting or scavenging bigger animals—might have been one of the requirements for expanding out of Africa. But the first sign of these large tools, known as Acheulean technology, comes from between 1.6 and 1.4 million years ago in Africa, a little *after* the first evidence of *Homo erectus* at Dmanisi and Java. Also, the thousands of stone tools found at Dmanisi are not Acheulean. Instead they are Oldowan pebble tools. The lack of large stone tools and the presence of small hominins at Dmanisi raises many questions about the roles that anatomy, behavior, and climate conditions played in the first human departures from Africa.

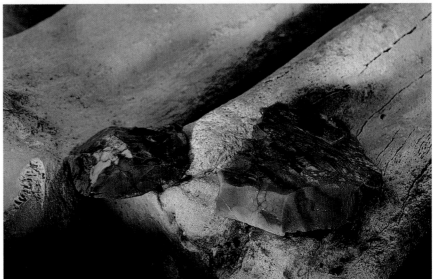

Large Acheulean hand axes, such as this one from Olorgesailie in Kenya (above, top), are often found miles away from the source of the stone used to make them. This suggests hominins were familiar with the landscape and local resources. In China such large tools are rare. Small sharp tools only an inch wide (above, bottom) are common, however. They were probably used to obtain meat from smaller animals.

Aside from Dmanisi, Africa, and Java, the best-known *Homo erectus* fossils are from China. In the 1920s, famous fossil specimens that came to be known as Peking Man were found not far from Beijing, the capital of China formerly called Peking, in a cave deposit at Zhoukoudian. Some specimens may have been 500,000 years old. Many of these important fossils were lost during World War II, and all attempts to find them since have failed. Fortunately, many new Chinese *Homo erectus* specimens and tools have been discovered since. One of them lived in China more than one million years ago.

By one million years ago early humans also had spread far west to Spain. Yet there, at Venta Micena, stone tools and animal bones are the only evidence of an early human presence. With no hominin fossils found there from that time period, we do not know what hominin made the tools. Fossil sites like Venta Micena, with tools and evidence of meat-eating and hunting, pepper the landscape of Europe, but again, it is difficult to say what hominin was there without human remains.

The earliest fossil human remains found in Europe are from about 780,000 years ago—long after the tools and animal bones were left at Venta Micena. These fossils were found at a site called Gran Dolina in north central Spain, along with hundreds of stone tools and the fossil remains of horses, rhinoceroses, wild cats, hyenas, and wolves.

Because so few fossils have been found, it is not completely clear what happened in the human lineage between 1.8 million and 200,000 years ago. There are, however, two leading models that scientists use to explain the existing fossil evidence. One is called the "out of Africa," or the "replacement," model, and the other is the "multiregional" model.

The replacement model proposes that *Homo ergaster*, the early African version of *Homo erectus*, left Africa around 1.8 to 1.7 million years ago and evolved outside Africa into *Homo erectus* and other closely-related species of humans. The *Homo ergaster* population that remained in Africa continued to evolve separately from those who left.

By one million years ago, this separate evolution had produced a population in Africa that had larger brains. These people are called archaic, meaning "ancient," *Homo sapiens*. According to the replacement model, some archaic *Homo sapiens* that evolved in Africa are the direct ancestors of anatomically modern humans—people with bodies like ours—which first appear in the fossil record in Africa about 200,000 years ago. These anatomically modern humans then expanded their range throughout the rest of Africa as well as out of Africa in a wave of emigration that swept through Europe and

Was it *Homo erectus* (artist's reconstruction, left) that abandoned tools at million-year-old sites outside Africa, such as Venta Micena in Spain (above)? We cannot be sure. The oldest well-dated human bones known from Europe are from Spain, but they are only 780,000 years old.

Asia. They competed with and replaced all other descendants of *Homo ergaster* everywhere.

Another, almost opposite, view is the multiregional model. In this model *Homo sapiens* and *Homo erectus* are really variations of the same hominin, captured in the fossil record at different evolutionary moments. This means that changes in *Homo* that evolved in one place were spread to many other places, a process that eventually produced anatomically modern humans everywhere. According to this model there were many opportunities for genes to be exchanged through mating among different groups of people over long periods of time. This would allow for genetic material to blend among them. "Multiregional" is the name given this model because it involves modern humans evolving in many regions of the world over time.

The multiregional model is useful to explain why we still find features that can be linked to *Homo erectus* in certain groups of modern humans. For example, the back of the incisor teeth (the ones you use to bite into a whole apple) are shovel-shaped in many Asians. This kind of tooth can be found in million-year-old Chinese specimens classified as *Homo erectus*. It also occurs, however, in some australopithecines. Another example is found among the Australian aborigines, who have distinctive faces with strong brow ridges and high cheek bones that are unique to them. Some scientists suggest these features are similar to those of the hominin now classified as late *Homo erectus* from Java. Both of these cases suggest that anatomically modern humans from Africa did not replace other species elsewhere. Instead, it suggests that the genes of early human groups that lived in various regions, including Africa, were mixed as modern humans evolved and are preserved in regional variations of human populations today.

In recent years, scientists have looked to our genes in an effort to test these differing ideas and to provide more evidence for when and where anatomically modern humans arose. Several kinds of genetic information are used in these studies. One type is called mitochondrial DNA because the genetic information comes from inside the mitochondria, a small energy-producing structure found in most human cells. Unlike many other kinds of genetic information, mitochondrial DNA is only passed on by mothers. Scientists can look at the mitochondrial DNA of

IRA BLOCK ▲

Many *Homo erectus* skulls from China, such as these two from Yunxian (left), have shovel-shaped incisors (above), just like many modern Asians.

The skull cap of the first *Homo erectus* found in Indonesia changed the way the world thought about human prehistory. The specimen is shown here among the study materials of their discoverer, Eugène Dubois, a Dutch physician who was convinced human ancestors could be found in Asia.

humans living around the world today and estimate how many generations of mothers have been passing along the original DNA, with occasional mutations, to their children. The Y chromosome is another part of our DNA that can be studied to track evolutionary history. This chromosome is only passed from fathers to male children. Like mitochondrial DNA, it can be used to estimate how many years it would take for the variety we see in the DNA of the Y chromosomes of males living today to evolve.

   Both mitochondrial DNA and the Y chromosome studies suggest that the genetic ancestors of all living humans lived somewhere south of the Sahara in Africa between 200,000 and 100,000 years ago. The reason for this is that the DNA of sub-Saharan Africans is easily recognized in the genomes of all living humans. It has a distinct pattern that is the result of its having been mixed and remixed among the peoples of that region over a long period of time.

Because Africans, such as this Masai boy in Tanzania, have a long history of exchanging genes in Africa, their genomes are highly varied and easily recognized. All other living human groups share this basic African set of genes, and only minor changes account for all of the human diversity we see today.

How could this occur? The replacement model proponents would say that this is what would be expected to occur if we all had started with African DNA. Proponents of the multi-regional model would say that perhaps Africa simply influenced our genome more than other regions because there were larger populations living there when modern humans were evolving.

The origin of modern humans is far from resolved. Evidence to support both views continues to be presented by scientists doing careful work on new fossil discoveries and our genomes. Much work remains to be done. For one thing, mitochondrial DNA and Y chromosomes are only two sets of genetic material. Other genetic studies suggest the most recent common ancestor of living humans lived not 100,000 or 200,000, but as many as two million years ago.

Wherever, however, and whenever modern humans originated, today we are all one species, *Homo sapiens*. We may look very different from each other on the surface, but our genes are almost identical, whether we are from Ethiopia or Iceland. There may be a hidden difference, however, between us and our ancestors of 100,000 years ago that bones alone cannot reveal. We may look the same as them, but did they behave as we do? To investigate this, we must go back and look at the immediate ancestors of *Homo sapiens* and how modern behavior emerged.

EARLY FOSSIL GENUS *Homo*

There is still much to learn about the origins of our own genus, *Homo*. Specimens called *Homo habilis*, the earliest known member of our genus, are so varied that scientists debate whether it is really one or several species. KNM-ER 1470 (below), for example, had a brain volume almost a third larger than KNM-ER 1813 *(see page 35)*. This and

Homo erectus or *Homo ergaster*
1.8 million years old, Kenya
fossil name: KNM-ER 3733

Homo habilis or *Homo rudolfensis*
1.8 to 1.9 million years old, Kenya
fossil name: KNM-ER 1470

other observations lead some scientists to reclassify KNM-ER 1470 as *Homo rudolfensis*. Others see reasons to reclassify KNM-ER 1813 as *Australopithecus habilis*.

Whatever the case, brain size is a crucial factor in identifying members of genus *Homo*. Generally, a member of *Homo*

should have a brain volume of more than 600 cubic centimeters. That's about the size of a big grapefruit.

The large-brained skull of what was most likely an adult female *Homo erectus* was found in Kenya in 1975 (above). It was about 1.8 million years old, which shows that our genus lived at the same time as other hominins. It is classified as *Homo erectus*, but some scientists suggest that it and

Homo erectus
400,000 to 500,000 years old, China
fossil name: PEKING MAN

other early African *Homo erectus* fossils should have their own species name of *Homo ergaster*.

Homo erectus was first discovered outside Africa on the island of Java in Indonesia and later in China. More recently, specimens have been found in Eurasia *(see page 38)*. Some scientists view certain early human fossils in Europe as *Homo erectus* as well, but there is much debate about their classification and age.

The Javan *Homo erectus* is remarkable for how long it lived

Homo erectus
800,000 years old, Indonesia
fossil name: SANGIRAN 17

there. There is evidence that *Homo erectus* lived in Java as early as 1.8 to 1.7 million years ago and as recently as 25,000 years ago.

China is also remarkable for its record of *Homo erectus*. No fewer than 40 individuals were found at just one site, the famous Zhoukoudian site near Beijing.

Years ago

Present

| 2,500,000 | 2,000,000 | 1,500,000 | 1,000,000 | 500,000 |

Homo habilis

Homo ergaster

Dmanisi Homo erectus

Homo erectus

Where are they found?
- Africa
- Eurasia
- Asia

CHAPTER FOUR

BECOMING MODERN

Becoming fully human as we are today had a lot to do with brain power. As the brains of our ancestors became bigger, humans became more creative and even better able to adjust rapidly to new conditions than they were before. The process of evolving into modern humans during the last million years was complex, however. Some scientists count as many as eight possible species in *Homo*, our genus, that lived during this time. And there is controversy about the origin of modern behavior, which ultimately led to our complex society today.

There was a noticeable increase in brain size that occurred around 700,000 years ago when a large hominin called archaic *Homo sapiens* evolved. Archaic *Homo sapiens* are

The origin of people who looked like modern humans (far right, and skeletons) was probably around 200,000 years ago. The origins of modern behaviors such as the making of figurines (near right) and complex tools (center right, bottom) are ancient as well, but just how ancient is still debated.

different from anatomically modern humans because they still had some ancestral features, such as enormous brow ridges and thick-walled bones. They are important because two of the largest brained humans ever—Neandertals and us—evolved from them. Some archaic *Homo sapiens* are also called *Homo heidelbergensis*—a name given because a jaw of this hominin type was found near Heidelberg in Germany. The reason some scientists make this distinction is that the archaic *Homo sapiens* in Europe are thought to be the ancestors of Neandertals, whereas others, such as those in Africa and Asia, are not.

One of the largest single deposits of any human fossils discovered anywhere was of *Homo heidelbergensis*. The remains of as many as 32 individuals were found at a 400,000-year-old site near Atapuerca in north central Spain. This spot is very near Gran Dolina, the site where the earliest hominin known from Europe, *Homo antecessor*, was found. Besides Atapuerca, however, physical remains of *Homo heidelbergensis* in Europe are somewhat sparse.

There are, however, many sites in Europe where early humans left their mark in other ways *(see page 40)*. The 400,000-year-old site of Terra Amata in France, for example, has some of the earliest known evidence of the controlled use of fire in hearths. At Torralba and Ambrona in Spain and at Bilzingsleben in Germany, the archaeological sites were littered with the bones of big animals and

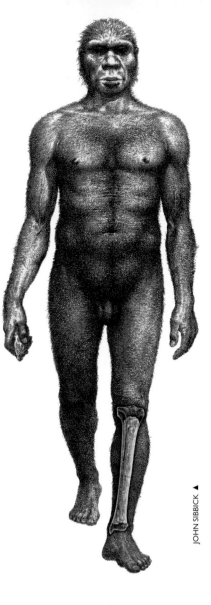

JOHN SIBBICK ▲

Scientists contemplate the sturdy brow of an early human fossil from Ceprano in Italy (left). Using bits of bone like this, and others, such as a leg bone from Boxgrove in the United Kingdom, an artist was able to reconstruct the possible appearance of the earliest known hominins in Europe (right). Many well-made stone hand axes (above) are associated with their remains.

hundreds of stone tools. The animals include carved-up elephants, rhinoceroses, horses, and deer. Scientists assume these were sites where *Homo heidelbergensis* was active, since it was the only hominin known to be in Europe during this time, but we cannot be sure.

By this time the Acheulean hand axe had evolved into a complex, symmetrical form that took great skill, planning, and a good chunk of time to make. Yet *Homo heidelbergensis* had something else in its toolkit that was, as far as we know, its innovation. This was the wooden spear. At the 500,000-year-old site of Boxgrove in southern England, a neat puncture hole in the shoulder blade of a butchered horse—the same shape that a spear would make—has scientists convinced

that spears were being used there. The earliest known actual spears come from Schöningen near Heidelberg, Germany. There, five wooden spears were found in amazingly good condition, considering that they were 400,000 years old. The spears had been cut from the branches of slow-growing trees, which produce the hardest wood possible, and then shaved to have sharp tips. The creation and use of new tools like these and the hunting of large prey suggests that *Homo heidelbergensis* was showing early signs of modern behavior. Hunting large animals successfully probably required group cooperation and complex planning—perhaps even some form of verbal communication, but we cannot be sure.

Outside Europe, archaic *Homo sapiens* fossils are known from Africa and Asia. In Africa, the archaic *Homo sapiens* are sometimes called *Homo rhodesiensis*, named after a well-preserved skull from Kabwe in Zambia, part of former Rhodesia. The bones of *Homo rhodesiensis* show that these humans were very large and strong. The males may have looked something like pro wrestlers today. The tools they used were similar to the Acheulean tools found in Europe, but thus far there is no evidence of wooden spears.

Asian archaic *Homo sapiens* had a different idea about tools than its European and African cousins. With few exceptions, such as the large hand axes found at Bose in China, tools found in Asia are small. There have been many explanations suggested for this difference in tool use. It could be that the earliest humans in Asia, *Homo erectus*, arrived with Oldowan technology before hand axes were invented—just like the people at Dmanisi. As they developed their stone tool-making industry, they might have included big hand axes, such as the ones at Bose, when they needed them. This scenario makes some sense as the hand axes from Bose were made using a different method from that used to make hand axes in the West.

Scientists have suggested another possible explanation for the general lack of hand axes in Asia. Hominins there may have used a different hard material than stone, such as the teeth of large animals or bamboo, to make their tools. Bamboo is still used in Asia today to make everything from shaving knives to cooking pots. Since it is extremely unlikely that bamboo would preserve as a fossil, we may never know if early humans made bamboo tools there or not.

As Asian hominins were pursuing their separate paths, so were hominins in Europe. A distinct lineage of humans—the Neandertals—evolved there, perhaps from *Homo heidelbergensis* and perhaps in response to geographical isolation.

Neandertals—or *Homo neanderthalensis*—were a group of humans that lived from about 225,000 years ago to 27,000 years ago in an area that stretched from Europe to western Asia. It is possible that the stout bodies of Neandertals were an advantage in a climate that included unusually cold temperatures. Stout bodies are an advantage for people who live in cold climates since a compact shape concentrates body temperature. Indeed the short, sturdy frames of Neandertals have been compared to those of native peoples living in cold regions near the poles today. But how well adapted to the cold Neandertals really were is unknown. It is possible that the extreme climates of this period contributed to their extinction.

How closely people living today are related to Neandertals is not agreed on. Were these stocky cousins of ours so different that they should be called a separate species, or were they so similar that they

Many Neandertal remains are found in caves, such as this one at Vindija in Croatia. The ice in the cave is a reminder that Neandertals endured periods of extremely cold climate. They are often compared to modern cold-adapted humans, such as the Inuit.

Life was rough for Neandertals. Many of their remains show the same type of injuries, such as broken arms and head injuries, that doctors see in rodeo riders. Perhaps this is because they hunted dangerous animals, such as this prehistoric ox known as an aurochs, at close range with sharp wooden stabbing spears.

interacted with our ancestors just as any two groups of humans would today? There is evidence to support both views.

Studies of genetic material from well-preserved Neandertal bones suggest that we and Neandertals are only distantly related and may even be separate species. Scientists found there was enough difference between a certain gene in the Neandertal material and the same gene in a modern human genome to say that each started on a separate evolutionary path as far back as 600,000 years ago.

Recently discovered fossil hominins from Ethiopia seem to support this view. Scientists suggest the 160,000-year-old remains show that humans there were already well on their way to evolving anatomically modern human features by that time. And they were making the transition from archaic *Homo sapiens* to anatomically modern *Homo sapiens* in Africa without any genetic mixing with Neandertals.

Modern human   Neandertal skull

HOW TO MAKE A
NEANDERTAL

Just how different from us did Neandertals look? Did their big brow ridge, receding chin, and large nose mean they would look alien to us? Computer experts at the Biomedical Visualization Laboratory at the University of Illinois at Chicago decided to find out.

First, scans of the well-preserved fossil skulls of a Neandertal male, female, and child were used to mark anatomical reference points such as the brow, nose, mouth, and chin. These same points were then plotted on the images of living models. These can be seen as green lines in the images above.

The computer program then "morphed" the faces of the modern humans to exactly match the reference points on the Neandertal bones, keeping in mind that there might be skin thickness differences between living humans and Neandertals. The result shows a dramatic difference, particularly in profile. The Neandertals' large brows, big noses, and jutting jaws show clearly. Yet it is impossible to look at them and not feel a kinship.

A 58,000-year-old Neandertal skull from Amud Cave in Israel (left) faces off with one of the earliest-known anatomically modern human fossils, a 92,000-year-old skull from nearby Qafzeh, also in Israel. These two groups overlapped in this region for tens of thousands of years.

On the other hand, a discovery in Portugal may support the idea that Neandertals and modern humans mixed genetically. It is the fossilized skeleton of a four-year-old child buried 25,000 years ago under a rock ledge near Lagar Velho. The burial would have been unremarkable except that the child showed signs that some scientists see as a mixture of both Neandertal and modern human features. It had stocky Neandertal limb bones but a smooth brow and the hint of a modern human chin. The child had been buried in the style of modern humans of that time: It was sprinkled with red ocher, probably wore a shell pendant and a headdress with deer teeth on it, and rabbit and deer bones were placed around its body.

Whether Neandertals are a separate species or more closely related to us, we have given them a bad reputation. When their fossil bones were found in Europe in the early 1800s, many people did not know what to make of them. In the late 1900s, a leading French scientist, Marcellin Boule, understood Neandertals as ancestors, but he described them as brutish, shuffling apemen. Only much later was it realized that the bones he had based his negative report on were those of a Neandertal that had been deformed by disease. Unfortunately, the bad image of Neandertals that Boule and others created has lasted more than a century.

In the last few decades scientists have been changing their view of Neandertals. One thing they point out is that Neandertals had big brains—bigger than the average modern human. And many scientists now give Neandertals credit for having compassion, partly based on evidence that they cared for their sick and elderly. Neandertals also buried their dead with antlers, tools, and other objects that may have been tokens of affection or a ritual belief.

Neandertals are also now given credit for being innovative. They had a set of tools that was more advanced than those of earlier hominins. These tools, which are sometimes called the

The results of an encounter between Neandertals and modern humans involves much speculation, but it is likely that they were aware of each other in Europe between 40,000 and 30,000 years ago. Would they have traded and shared knowledge as shown in this artist's depiction, or would they have been hostile toward each other? It's anyone's guess.

Mousterian toolkit, were used to perform a variety of jobs, such as scraping hides or bark, slicing meat, and chopping wood. A single Mousterian tool could be shaped so each of its sides was useful for different purposes—like a prehistoric Swiss army knife.

Mousterian tools can be found all over Europe and western Asia *(see page 64)*. They were also found in the caves of northern Israel, which were occupied by prehistoric humans between 120,000 and 40,000 years ago. Some caves excavated in this area, such as at Amud, contained the bones of Neandertals, and others, such as the Qafzeh site, contained the bones of some of the earliest known anatomically modern *Homo sapiens*. Yet there is no evidence that they lived there at the same time.

The early *Homo sapiens* at Qafzeh and other sites look similar to some modern humans, yet their remains were found only with Mousterian tools. Their tools suggest that their behavior was like that of Neandertals. To some scientists this suggests that the *Homo sapiens* at Qafzeh simply *looked* modern and should be distinguished from humans that *behaved* in a modern way. This is the reason *anatomically* modern humans are sometimes distinguished from *behaviorally* modern humans.

To some scientists this confusing picture from northern Israel is easily explained. In their view, the appearance of both modern human and Neandertal skeletons there simply shows a transition between Neandertals and modern humans. This view is consistent with the multiregional model that suggests that anatomically modern humans were evolving as genes were passed between many groups living in Europe, Africa, and Asia at that time.

On the other hand, proponents of the replacement model see the Neandertals in northern Israel as a separate species from the anatomically modern humans there. In their view,

Before Neandertals disappeared around 27,000 years ago, their tools (above left) started changing to look similar to those of their behaviorally modern neighbors (left object of above right pair). Some even adorned themselves with necklaces of drilled animal teeth (right object of above right pair). The pace of change set by the modern humans was rapid and included everything from harpoon tips for spearing fish (above, pictured with fish) to throwing spears, carved figures, and sewing needles.

Cave walls at Altamira in Spain were painted with natural pigments made from iron oxide, chalk, and charcoal about 15,000 years ago but look like they were painted yesterday. Other paintings, such as those in the Coa Valley of Portugal, have not fared so well because they were painted outdoors on large rock surfaces.

while Neandertals were evolving from *Homo heidelbergensis* in Europe, anatomically modern humans evolved separately from archaic *Homo sapiens* in Africa.

This does not explain, however, why the early anatomically modern humans at Qafzeh and other sites in Israel were behaving like Neandertals. Again, there are differing points of view about the explanation for this. One idea is that modern behavior was the result of a genetic mutation that caused brain "rewiring" around 50,000 years ago. The result was a behavioral revolution—the rapid spreading through the population of a greater ability for creative thinking. This had not yet occurred among the early modern humans living in Israel.

Another view is that no dramatic genetic mutations are needed to explain why the people at Qafzeh used Neandertal-like tools. It may be that they simply did not need anything else. Supporting this view is evidence that modern human behavior in the form of tool-making, fishing, and the use of ocher, for example, was occurring here and there in Africa much earlier than 50,000 years ago. It is possible that anatomically modern humans were gradually developing modern behavior in Africa over hundreds of thousands of years and that during this time they behaved in a "modern" way only when they needed to. Eventually it was these forms of behavior that dramatically distinguished *Homo sapiens* from Neandertals. In particular, it was the degree to which *Homo sapiens* practiced these behaviors that made the difference.

A hungry bear interrupts a hunting party of modern humans who chanced across a mammoth carcass. They will use the skin, meat, bone, and ivory for food, clothing, tools, art, and shelter. They probably depended more on smaller game, such as rabbits, foxes, and birds caught with rope nets, for their regular fare.

GREGORY MANCHESS

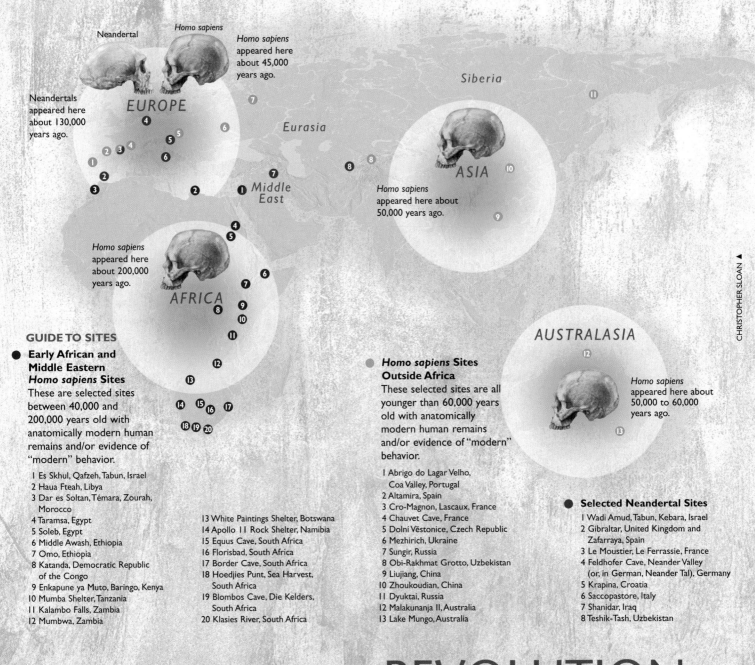

Neandertal

Homo sapiens

Homo sapiens appeared here about 45,000 years ago.

Neandertals appeared here about 130,000 years ago.

EUROPE

④

⑤
④

② ③ ④
⑤
⑥

① ⑥

②

③

② ①

Eurasia

Middle East
⑦

Siberia

⑪

⑦

⑧ ⑧

ASIA

⑩

⑨

Homo sapiens appeared here about 50,000 years ago.

Homo sapiens appeared here about 200,000 years ago.

AFRICA

④
⑤

⑥
⑦

⑨
⑧
⑩

⑪

⑫

⑬

⑭ ⑮ ⑰
⑯
⑱ ⑲ ⑳

AUSTRALASIA

⑫

⑬

Homo sapiens appeared here about 50,000 to 60,000 years ago.

CHRISTOPHER SLOAN ▲

GUIDE TO SITES

● **Early African and Middle Eastern *Homo sapiens* Sites**
These are selected sites between 40,000 and 200,000 years old with anatomically modern human remains and/or evidence of "modern" behavior.

1 Es Skhul, Qafzeh, Tabun, Israel
2 Haua Fteah, Libya
3 Dar es Soltan, Témara, Zourah, Morocco
4 Taramsa, Egypt
5 Soleb, Egypt
6 Middle Awash, Ethiopia
7 Omo, Ethiopia
8 Katanda, Democratic Republic of the Congo
9 Enkapune ya Muto, Baringo, Kenya
10 Mumba Shelter, Tanzania
11 Kalambo Falls, Zambia
12 Mumbwa, Zambia

13 White Paintings Shelter, Botswana
14 Apollo 11 Rock Shelter, Namibia
15 Equus Cave, South Africa
16 Florisbad, South Africa
17 Border Cave, South Africa
18 Hoedjies Punt, Sea Harvest, South Africa
19 Blombos Cave, Die Kelders, South Africa
20 Klasies River, South Africa

● ***Homo sapiens* Sites Outside Africa**
These selected sites are all younger than 60,000 years old with anatomically modern human remains and/or evidence of "modern" behavior.

1 Abrigo do Lagar Velho, Coa Valley, Portugal
2 Altamira, Spain
3 Cro-Magnon, Lascaux, France
4 Chauvet Cave, France
5 Dolní Věstonice, Czech Republic
6 Mezhirich, Ukraine
7 Sungir, Russia
8 Obi-Rakhmat Grotto, Uzbekistan
9 Liujiang, China
10 Zhoukoudian, China
11 Dyuktai, Russia
12 Malakunanja II, Australia
13 Lake Mungo, Australia

● **Selected Neandertal Sites**
1 Wadi Amud, Tabun, Kebara, Israel
2 Gibraltar, United Kingdom and Zafarraya, Spain
3 Le Moustier, Le Ferrassie, France
4 Feldhofer Cave, Neander Valley (or, in German, Neander Tal), Germany
5 Krapina, Croatia
6 Saccopastore, Italy
7 Shanidar, Iraq
8 Teshik-Tash, Uzbekistan

WAS THERE A BEHAVIOR REVOLUTION?

Abundant evidence of modern human behavior at European sites that are 45,000 years old or younger suggests to some scientists that this behavior may have evolved suddenly, in what has been called a behavioral revolution. According to others there may have been no revolution at all. These scientists suggest that a focus on evidence in Europe—ignoring Africa— gives a false impression of a revolution. They argue that, as this map shows, there are numerous older sites in Africa and the Middle East with anatomically modern human remains and/or evidence of "modern" behavior. They suggest that humans in Africa had been practicing many of the innovations that are commonly associated with modern behavior long before they expanded out of the region about 60,000 years ago. These activities include making finely worked projectile points that differ in design from region to region, trading over long distances for stone to make certain tools, and making implements, such as harpoons, from bone.

Most evidence points to modern human origins being somewhere in Africa between 100,000 and 200,000 years ago. The footprints of someone who could very well have been an ancestor to us all were preserved in the sand near what is now Hoedjies Punt at the southern tip of Africa 100,000 years ago.

What were these new behaviors that set *Homo sapiens* apart? They were the ability to think abstractly, to make complex plans, to be innovative, and to use symbols. The list of how modern humans expressed these behaviors is long.

Among the most obvious new activities of modern humans was an increased attention to culture. Part of the evidence for this is that their behavior went beyond the practical needs of everyday life. People began to show an appreciation for the beauty of things. They started decorating themselves with jewelry made of animal teeth and bits of ostrich egg shells. Some of these items came from far away, suggesting long-distance travel or trade and the planning that would take. They buried each other with these items as well and sprinkled graves with red ocher powder. This is a possible indication of abstract thinking since burial rituals are often about caring for the dead in an afterlife—something the living cannot see.

Around 40,000 years ago humans started making elaborate art. They carved bone and antler into familiar animals as well as fantastic ones and painted and carved rocks in caves and canyons. One of the oldest examples of cave art is from Chauvet Cave in France, which contains paintings over 30,000 years old. Prehistoric artists drew cave lions and cave bears lurking, mammoths and rhinoceroses parading, and huge wild oxen called aurochs charging.

The technological innovations of modern humans are no less impressive than their art. The technology included the use of ivory, antler, and bone for complex tools such as harpoons, fishhooks, sewing needles, and awls. They also produced more intricate forms of stone tools, such as those carefully formed with thin blades of stone instead of flakes. The blades, at least twice as long as they were wide, were attached to wood—or hafted—to make spears, axes, and eventually arrows. Raw materials to make tools, such as obsidian and flint, were transported many miles and were probably even traded between groups of people. Rope making from plant material may have been among the innovations as well. The impression of fiber in hardened clay from Mezhirich, a 28,000-year-old campsite in the Ukraine, suggests that perhaps nets were being made long ago to catch fish as well as small birds and mammals.

If we assume for a moment that there was no genetic mutation to drive a behavioral revolution 50,000 years ago, then what could it have been? An all-too-human explanation is that maybe people only found it necessary to change their behavior when social, environmental, or population pressures over time forced them to.

Was there something that happened between 100,000 and 50,000 years ago that could have forced such a change? Possibly. Environmental change brought on by increasingly frequent changes in global temperature or a climate-changing natural disaster, such as a volcanic eruption, could have been a source of pressure that forced people to adopt new behavior. For example, a colder climate could have led to sewn clothing and tent shelters.

Survival in difficult times may also have depended on improved communication. It was probably an advantage for people to talk to each other to make plans. Once speech got started, it may have become the main force in pushing further brain growth. People who communicated better than others probably made more attractive mates and were thus more likely to pass on their genes.

During the last 10,000 years, the pace of creative expression and invention among humans continued to increase. The stone and bone tools that humans had used for millions of years gave way to metals; wild animals were tamed; and grains, fruits, and vegetables were grown on farms. Humans were now set on a course that would lead us to have a major impact on the Earth—and on ourselves.

Early artists in the Ukraine experimented with engraving a piece of mammoth tooth into a human likeness on this 15,000-year-old plaque.

Homo heidelbergensis
250,000 years old, Germany
fossil name: STEINHEIM

LATER *Homo*

The path to our modern physical form is anything but clear, yet there are many fossil clues and theories about how it all happened. One of the most controversial issues is whether *Homo sapiens*—our species—evolved and eventually replaced all other hominins, or if there was a global blending of genes that led to our species evolving everywhere more or less at the same time.

Key players in this process are *Homo heidelbergensis* (left) and archaic *Homo sapiens* (below left). Some scientists view these two as species that evolved later in two different directions; *Homo heidelbergensis* led to Neandertals (*Homo neanderthalensis*, right) and archaic *Homo sapiens*, at least the African form also known as *Homo rhodesiensis*, led to *Homo sapiens* (below right).

Genetic studies and new African fossil finds, such as *Homo sapiens idaltu*, a hominin that has both archaic and anatomically modern *Homo sapiens* features, suggest that Neandertals and modern humans went their separate ways genetically about 600,000 years ago. Many scientists see this evidence as strong support for the view that *Homo sapiens* evolved in Africa and then completely replaced the Neandertals and any other hominins that still lived. This view, however, is still debated.

Homo neanderthalensis
or Homo sapiens neanderthalensis
58,000 years old, Israel
fossil name: AMUD 1

Archaic *Homo sapiens* or
Homo rhodesiensis
500,000 years old, Zambia
fossil name: KABWE or BROKEN HILL

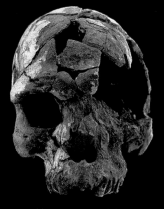

Homo sapiens idaltu
160,000 years old, Ethiopia
fossil name: BOU-VP-16/1

National Museum of Ethiopia, Addis Ababa
© 2001 David L. Brill/Brill Atlanta

Anatomically modern
Homo sapiens
92,000 years old, Israel
fossil name: QAFZEH IX

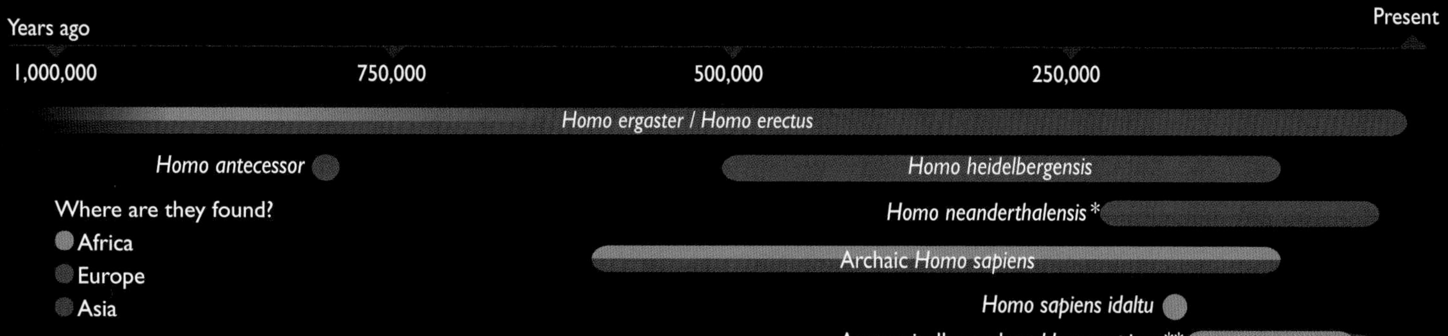

Years ago
Present

1,000,000   750,000   500,000   250,000

Homo ergaster / Homo erectus

Homo antecessor

Homo heidelbergensis

Where are they found?

Homo neanderthalensis *

● Africa

● Europe
Archaic *Homo sapiens*

● Asia
Homo sapiens idaltu ●

Anatomically modern *Homo sapiens* **

* Neandertals are known as far east as Uzbekistan, but no farther.
** Behaviorally modern humans are shown here in blue emerging around 50,000 years ago.

CHAPTER FIVE

BEING HUMAN TODAY

It has been 11,500 years since the end of the last major ice age. That is a very short time compared to the six million years or so since our first human ancestors appeared. But in that short time, humans have done something truly extraordinary. We have stood evolution on its head.

For millions of years the adaptations that determined the success or failure of our species were acquired naturally, through natural selection. If evolution had not equipped a plant or animal with what it needed to survive and reproduce, it went extinct. But ever since the origins of modern human behavior, humans have been able to adapt to new environments and conditions with great rapidity—not biologically, but through technology.

The first modern humans did not wait for evolution to produce adaptations, they invented them. Warm hearths, sewn clothing, and shelters made colder environments livable. Harpoons, fish hooks, and nets made fish and small mammals easier to catch. And when a resource was scarce, such as a certain type of stone to make a tool, they were able to trade for it or

Equipped with modern behavior, humans at the end of the last ice age continued their innovations as their population grew. Many swapped a nomadic life in tents (right) for permanent housing and started to raise animals and crops.

68

travel long distances to get it themselves. This is not to say that natural selection was not still a force that affected humans. It certainly was and still is. It is just that our big brains had made us one of the most adaptable creatures on the planet.

At the end of the last ice age, the pace of our technological adaptations began increasing. This was because civilization—people living in groups in villages and towns—began. Changes for humans have been more sudden and dramatic since the beginning of civilization than during any other period of hominin history.

Almost one quarter of the Earth's land surface, particularly in the northern continents, was under ice when the last ice age hit its peak about 18,000 years ago. As climate changed, new areas suitable for humans became available. The thawing took more than 2,000 years, but as moisture was freed by the melting ice it poured into rivers and rained onto dry areas, turning them into woodlands and fertile meadows.

During this climate change, some people began to shift from a life of hunting and gathering to settling permanently. Gradually they began to raise animals and tend plants. The shift to agriculture and herding was aided by the changes in climate that produced new habitable areas, but increasing population and dwindling numbers of easily caught prey were other factors that probably forced people to find new ways to support themselves. The earliest known permanent settlements were built as part of this shift to an agricultural lifestyle.

Scientists have a good record of how this happened in the Middle East, where people of a culture we call Natufian lived between 13,000 and 10,500 years ago—right when the world's ice sheets were thawing. They built small villages of circular homes with stone walls. Some scientists interpret the archaeological remains found around their dwellings, such as grinding stones and stone sickles, to mean that the Natufians were changing from a lifestyle of hunting and gathering to practicing a primitive form of agriculture. They were among the first groups of people to discover that large-seeded grasses—the ancestors of modern barley and wheat—could be spread and cultivated deliberately.

People discovered the benefits of an agricultural lifestyle independently and at different times around the world. The secrets to growing rice were discovered by people living in the fertile river valleys of Pakistan, India, and China sometime around 7,000 years ago. People in the New World grew squash as early as 10,000 years ago and maize—or corn—as early as 4,000 years ago.

Art painted long ago on rock walls in the Kakadu National Park of Australia recalls the energetic life of hunter-gatherers. Their lifestyle was probably not something we would want to go back to, but many people today might actually benefit from a diet and exercise level more like theirs.

As towns and villages grew, so did the numbers of domesticated animals, as these wooden models prepared for an ancient Egyptian's tomb show. Animals were not only useful as food but as extra muscle power for heavy work, such as pulling carts and plows. Working animals, along with help from other villagers, improved a farmer's ability to grow enough food to store some for protection against future hard times.

Many early farmers continued to hunt animals for meat. Eventually, they learned that certain animals could be domesticated. These animals, which included pigs, sheep, goats, and cattle, were selected partly because they were less dangerous than other animals and also because their natural instincts made them easy for humans to control. In Africa cattle herders thrived in the Sahara, which at the end of the ice ages was a fertile area with rivers, lakes, and vegetation. They lived there until about 4,500 years ago, when arid conditions returned and buried everything under hundreds of feet of sand.

One big advantage of an agricultural lifestyle was security. Being in a group that stored food protected individuals from starvation. Villages also provided protection from being raided by other humans. People found that working together was useful for successfully accomplishing big tasks such as building homes, plowing, harvesting, and guarding herds.

Though our ability to artificially adapt has helped us, there are ways in which we may have gotten ahead of ourselves. Some modern health problems are now being linked to the fact

that our bodies, which are still the same physically as the bodies of hunter-gatherers of the last ice age, are exposed to influences we have not physically evolved to combat.

For example, a whole range of diseases came with the emergence of agriculture. These diseases were transmitted by pathogens, such as viruses, parasites, and bacteria. Living in villages at close quarters with livestock made it easier for pathogens to pass between animals and humans. Lack of knowledge about proper trash and sewage disposal or ways to preserve food and fresh water brought unsanitary conditions that provided breeding grounds for microbes, and living close together let diseases spread easily. Parasitic worms, dysentery, plague, and contagious diseases such as measles, tuberculosis, and influenza are just a few diseases that came along with our agricultural lifestyle.

Countless recent advances in medicine and improvements in public health due to better sanitation and nutrition have provided ways of dealing with many of these diseases. The result is that most modern humans live longer than our ancestors did. From what we can tell from the fossil record, the average life expectancy for ice-age men was around 35 years and for women, 30. Things did not improve dramatically until modern

Hunter-gatherers arrived in the Americas 12,500 years ago or even earlier. In these new lands they encountered abundant wildlife. In this scene, people prepare hunting and fishing tools near pools that today are part of the Aucilla River in Florida. Their prey might have included the tapirs, horses, and mastadons that lived there.

73

times. In some countries today, such as Singapore, Switzerland, and Sweden, the average life expectancy is 77 years.

Yet even this apparent progress has a downside. Since people today commonly live twice as long as ice-age humans did, our bodies are pushed way beyond the years our genes are programmed for. The result is that many parts of our bodies simply give out like the parts of an old car, causing many predictable problems as we get older. Longer lives combined with unhealthy eating and exercise habits are at least partly responsible for what seems like a modern plague of illnesses that affect older people, such as cancers, heart diseases, and senility.

Scientists who specialize in the new field of evolutionary medicine point to the transition to agriculture as being responsible for some of our diet-related health problems as well. They suggest that during our hunting and gathering days, which make up by far the majority of our history, we evolved bodies and body systems that were suited to that lifestyle and not to how most of us live today. It is possible that some types of mental illness, allergies, reproductive disorders, obesity, high blood pressure, and age-related ailments result from this mismatch.

Our diet has changed dramatically since hunter-gatherer days. Our ice-age ancestors depended on the natural food supply around them, which included the lean meat of wild animals and an assortment of fruits, vegetables, and nuts. Since these resources were not always dependable, it was an evolutionary advantage in good times for humans to be able to consume lots of extra calories, the energy units produced from food. These calories were stored in fat that could then be burned when less food was available.

Our bodies still process food—and store calories in fat—as if we were hunter-gatherers. Yet not only do we not live like hunter-gatherers, but half of what people in developed countries eat today are foods that were not available until after the ice age, when our ancestors settled down to farm. The new foods included modern grains, dairy products, sugar, alcohol, and processed fats such as vegetable oil. On top of this, domesticated animals are deliberately fattened, often on starchy grains, to produce meat that is much more fatty than the wild prey hunter-gatherers ate.

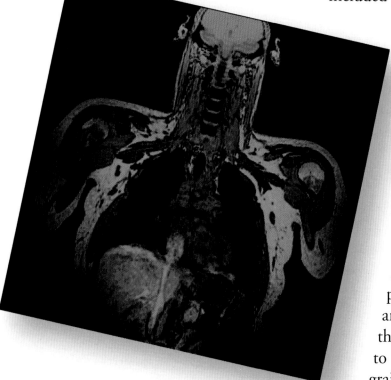

As our bodies process food we stow away fuel for future use as fat. If we do not burn it up it sits in large deposits, seen as light orange areas in this image, and can cause major health problems.

All of this access to calorie-packed foods would not be a problem except that the lean times to burn fat never come. So many people do not use up the calories they consume. Carrying too much fat in your body (obesity) is a cause of several health problems, including high blood pressure, diabetes, gall-bladder disease, heart disease, and osteoarthritis. In North America and Europe, almost one third of the population is now obese, and obesity is rapidly becoming a health concern in developing countries as well.

In our quest to be a more and more successful species, we have overwhelmed not only ourselves, but the rest of the living world. As human society became more complex, our need for raw materials, such as metals, increased. New tools made from these metals made humans more effective than ever at clearing forests for farmland, housing, and fuel. As a result of this and many other effects of civilization, such as pollution, humans have damaged the natural environment and endangered or caused the extinction of many other species. We are jeopardizing our future by using up nonrenewable resources, reducing freshwater sources through consumption and pollution, and perhaps even causing changes in climate.

Now we are looking at how we have damaged the Earth and are trying to fix what we can. We are asking ourselves hard questions about how to go about it. Often the needs of humans and those of the natural environment seem to be at odds.

Humans are at a crossroads. We have become expert at adapting to our environment or changing the environment to suit our needs, but we now may be able to go a step further. We can steer our own biological

Cerebral cortex

Ventricles

Hippocampus

The brain loses as much as 10 percent of its prime adult weight by age 90. The hippocampus, an area critical to memory, is also affected. Changes in the ventricles may be connected with slowing reactions and faltering memory as well.

Much of what was once considered to be a normal part of aging is now known to be the result of disease and unhealthy lifestyles. Many other effects of aging, such as the loss of brain tissue, hearing, bone and muscle mass, and the deterioration of vision and cartilage in our joints, happen because we are living longer than our ancestors. These problems often start in our thirties or forties—what would have been considered a ripe old age for our ice-age ancestors.

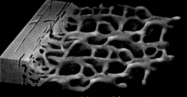

Normal bone tissue

Porous bone tissue

It is normal for bone cells to die and be replaced by new ones. Around age 35, however, more bone cells are lost than are replaced. This eventually results in bones that are porous and brittle, and therefore easily broken.

evolution. Science has advanced to the point where we have a map of our own genome and will likely be able to manipulate it directly.

As they study the genome, scientists will discover the causes of many genetically related disorders. Forty percent of adults today have genes that make it more likely for them to get a variety of common diseases. In developing countries genetic disorders account for the deaths of almost one in every four infants between the ages of one and four. Doctors armed with genetic information are already attacking many medical problems, including those associated with aging. Over 9,000 disorders caused by mutations in single genes have already been identified.

Eventually it will be possible to spot trouble in genomes and fix them long before they cause harm. Manipulation of genes will make it possible for more people to have normal lives. This is a truly wonderful thing, but it is definitely not normal. No species has ever been able to repair its own genome before.

Genetic manipulation raises the possibility that permanent changes can be made and thus may be passed on to our children. But this power to alter our own genes—and in effect guide our own evolution—raises huge questions for humanity. If we move too quickly it will be like operating a car when we have not yet learned how to drive.

Surely there is good reason for medicine to move as rapidly as it can to save lives through correcting genetic disorders, but it will be tempting to use genetic manipulation to do more than correct health problems. Where do we draw the line? It will be possible for parents to have complete control not only over their children's health—or rather, future health—but their physical features as well. It will be possible for parents to select sex, hair color, eye color, and many other characteristics before birth. Even the genetic recipes for intellect, social skills, and athletic ability might be available someday.

A genetically manipulated future will be far from problem free. Aside from questions about whether it is right or wrong to interfere with nature and who should make those decisions, there are health concerns. Our experience with breeding animals provides one of the most obvious examples. When we breed animals, we are intervening in natural selection and making our own decisions about which animals will reproduce. This human-guided evolution, which has produced everything from basset hounds and hairless cats to Lippizan stallions and Texas longhorn cattle, is called artificial selection. In some cases we have bred domesticated animals to the point that they are not physically fit. In the case of dogs, boxers can no longer breathe well through their noses, and German shepherds, golden retrievers, and dobermans suffer from crippling joint problems. Bulldogs cannot even breed without human assistance. Without firm guidelines, future humans could manipulate themselves into genetic corners as well.

Should we take this next step into the realm of manipulating our own evolution? No other species has ever come this far, but no other species has ever asked what is right, either. With our newfound understanding of the world and the amazing technologies we have developed since the beginning of civilization, we now have the ability to fix many of the problems we face. Yet if we ignore how intimately our well-being is linked to the health of this planet, then we will surely be the masters of nothing but our own extinction.

We must remember that it took millions of years for our species to evolve to what we are today. We are fortunate to be able to reflect on our history and prehistory like no generation before us and to use our knowledge to help us make good decisions for tomorrow. The future experience not only of humanity, but of all life on Earth, is now in the hands of a clever bipedal ape with a big brain.

Physical traits that make us look different from each other are influenced in very complex ways by inherited genes. Genetic manipulation could make us all look the same, but genetic differences, even if they are extremely small, make a species strong.

Glossary

Acheulean (ASH-oo-lay-en) A prehistoric stone tool type that includes large hand-held axes that have had chips flaked off on both sides. Named for the site St. Acheul in France.

adaptation Any change in structure, function, or behavior that enables an organism to be more successful in its environment. Adaptations are the result of the evolutionary process, particularly natural selection.

archaeology The scientific study of people that lived in the past through what remains of their culture, such as artifacts, dwellings, etc.

artificial selection In contrast to natural selection (see definition), this is a process in which adaptations or genetic traits are deliberately selected by humans. The most common examples of this are found in agriculture or among pets and gardening, where "unnatural" forms of plants and animals are considered desirable.

australopithecine Any member of the genus *Australopithecus*.

bipedal Walking on two legs.

DNA Letters standing for deoxyribonucleic acid. DNA is found in the nucleus of cells. It forms long strings of chemical pairs called nucleotides in the shape of a double helix. These form chromosomes. DNA plays a key role in the transfer of genetic information.

chromosomes Stringlike bodies within a cell nucleus that contain DNA and other material important for the transfer of genetic instructions during cell division. Humans have 23 pairs of chromosomes.

evolution Change in the inherited characteristics of groups of organisms. Over many generations this may result in new species.

gene A specific sequence of base pairs in DNA that can influence inherited traits.

genome The full DNA sequence of an organism. In humans, the DNA from all 23 chromosome pairs.

hominid, hominin See explanation page 14.

human In this book the word human refers to all members of our lineage since our last common ancestor with chimpanzees. "Anatomically modern humans" are those whose bodies are like ours today. "Behaviorally modern" or "fully modern" human refers to people just like us.

ice age A time when the world's climate is cold and glaciers cover most of the Earth. This happens periodically. The last major glaciation began around 110,000 years ago and ended about 11,500 years ago.

mitochondria A structure found outside the nucleus of a cell that provides fuel to the cell. It also contains DNA, although it is not used in reproduction.

Mousterian (moose-TAIR-ee-yen) A prehistoric stone tool type associated with Neandertals and some anatomically modern humans. In general, this technology involved more use of flakes—or chips—and the cores the flakes were broken from. Named for the site Le Moustier in France.

natural selection Greater reproductive success among particular members of a species because they have characteristics that give them an advantage in a particular environment. Successful animals and plants survive and reproduce, thus producing a new generation with a greater percentage of the favored feature. Charles Darwin coined this term, and it is the central mechanism in his theory of evolution.

Neandertal (nee-AN-dur-tall) Humans that lived between approximately 225,000 and 27,000 years ago. Their range stretched from Europe to Western Asia. The word comes from the Neander Valley of Germany where they were first found.

Oldowan (OL-doh-wahn) A prehistoric stone tool type produced by striking stones together to produce simple sharp flakes. The name comes from Olduvai Gorge in Tanzania.

paleoanthropology The scientific study of prehistoric humans.

paranthropine Any member of the genus *Paranthropus*. This group is made up of hominins with extra-large molars and jaw muscles. They are sometimes called the robust australopithecines.

paleontology The scientific study of prehistoric life.

sexual selection This is an important part of the natural selection process. In order to reproduce and pass on genes, most living things must successfully mate. Those that evolve traits or behaviors that make it more likely that they will be the ones to mate have been "sexually selected."

trait Any specific characteristic of an organism that is expressed through genes.

HOW DO WE KNOW WHAT PREHISTORIC HOMININS LOOKED LIKE?

Making pictures or sculptures of prehistoric life is called reconstruction. This is because the artists that do this literally have to put the past together bit by bit. Sometimes a single artwork involves the input of several scientists: one for the hominins, one for other animals, one for plants, etc. Many times, because the artist is working with fossils, there is not much to go on. This illustration of *Homo habilis* specimen OH 62, for instance, is based on the few bits of bone that the artist has shown in dark brown on the skeleton. Everything else, including the missing parts of skeletons, flesh and flesh color, hairiness, age of the individual, and eyes, are carefully worked out based on what we know about other hominins as well as living apes and humans.

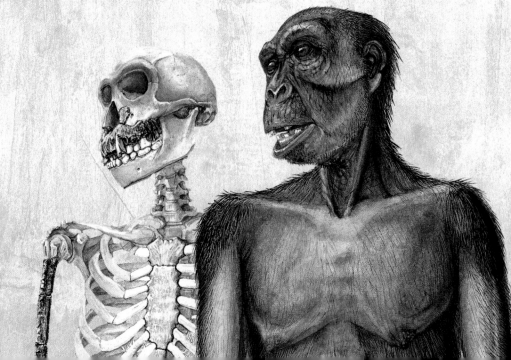

PORTIA SLOAN ▲

Pronunciations

Many names of species and places in the world of paleoanthropology are real tongue twisters that even scientists do not pronounce consistently. Here is a list of pronunciations of some of the tougher words in this book.

HOMININS

Sahelanthropus (SAW-hell-AN-throw-puss)
  tchadensis (chad-EN-sis)
Orrorin (Or-OR-in)
  tugenensis (too-gen-EN-sis)
Ardipithecus (AHR-dih-PITH-ih-cuss)
  ramidus (RAM-ih-duss)
Australopithecus
    (Aw-STRAL-oh-PITH-ih-cuss)
  anamensis (AN-uh-MEN-sis)
  afarensis (AH-far-EN-sis)
  africanus (AH-free-KAHN-uss)
  bahrelghazali (BAH-rell-gah-ZAH-lee)
Kenyanthropus (ken-YAN-throw-puss)
  platyops (PLAT-ee-ops)
Paranthropus (puh-RAN-throw-puss)
  boisei (BOY-zee-eye)
  aethiopicus (ee-thee-OH-pih-cuss)
  robustus (roh-BUST-us)
Homo (HOE-moe)
  habilis (HAB-ih-liss)
  rudolfensis (ROO-dawlf-EN-sis)
  erectus (ee-RECT-us)
  ergaster (uhr-GAST-urh)
  antecessor (ANT-ih-cess-sir)
  heidelbergensis (HIE-dull-burg-EN-sis)
  neanderthalensis
    (nee-AND-uhr-tall-EN-sis)
  sapiens (SAY-pee-enz)

PLACES

Afar (AH-far)
Aramis (AIR-uuh-miss)
Bilzingsleben (BILLS-zings-lay-ben)
Chauvet (show-VAY)
Dmanisi (dih-min-NEE-see)
Hadar (HAH-dahr)
Olorgesailie
  (oh-LORE-gih-SIGH-lee)
Nariokotome
  (NAR-ee-oh-KO-tow-may)
Olduvai
  (OLD-oo-vigh. Rhymes with sigh.)
Qafzeh (COUGH-zay)
Schöningen (SHUR-ning-gen)
Ubeidiya (oo-beh-DEE-yuh)
Yunxian (YOON-shen)
Zhoukoudian (JO-koo-dee-YEN)

Bibliography

Visualizing the past has been a passion of mine since a very early age. I remember being thrilled to receive a National Geographic Society book called *Wild Animals of North America* from my grandparents as a gift when I was only six. In its pages were wonderful photographs and illustrations of animals. My favorites were the prehistoric scenes, particularly the one of prehistoric humans fighting a cave bear by André Duranceau (right). I identified with the wide-eyed kid in the lower left-hand corner of the painting.

Little did I know that years later I would work at *National Geographic Magazine* and have a job that involves working with the talented artists, photographers, writers, and scientists who make subjects like prehistory so exciting. Now that cave bear painting is hanging on a wall in my office that faces my desk. Every day I look at it and hope that I have been successful in getting at least one kid out there as excited about this subject as I am.

Here are some books, magazine articles, and websites that I think might be interesting to anyone who wants to do some further reading on this subject.

Books

Bahn, P. G., and Vertut, J. *Journey Through the Ice Age*. University of California Press, Berkeley and Los Angeles, 1997.

Burenhult, G., editor. *People of the Stone Age: Hunter-Gatherers and Early Farmers*. American Museum of Natural History. Harper, San Francisco, 1993.

Burenhult, G., editor. *People of the Stone Age: Human Origins and History to 10,000 B.C.* American Museum of Natural History. Harper, San Francisco, 1993.

Johanson, D., Johanson, L., and Edgar, B. *Ancestors: In Search of Human Origins*. Random House, New York, 1994.

Johanson, D. and Edgar, B. *From Lucy to Language*. Simon & Schuster, New York, 1996.

Scarre, C., editor. *Past Worlds: Atlas of Archaeology*. HarperCollins, Ann Arbor, 2001.

Schick, K., and Toth, N.. *Making Silent Stones Speak*. Simon & Schuster, New York, 1993.

Stanford, C. B.. *The Hunting Apes*. Princeton University Press, Princeton, 1999.

ANDRÉ DURANCEAU ▲

Prehistoric humans fight a huge bear in *Wild Animals of North America*.

Articles in *National Geographic*
(In chronological order)

Leakey, Meave. *Dawn of Humans: The Farthest Horizon*. September 1995.

Gore, Rick. *Dawn of Humans: Neandertals*. January 1996.

Johanson, Donald. C. *Dawn of Humans. Face-to-Face with Lucy's Family*. March 1996.

Gore, Rick. *Dawn of Humans: The First Steps*. February 1997.

Gore, Rick. *Dawn of Humans: Expanding Worlds*. May 1997.

Gore, Rick. *Dawn of Humans: The First Europeans*. July 1997.

Gore, Rick. *Dawn of Humans: Tracking the First of Our Kind*. September 1997.

Gore, Rick. *Dawn of Humans: Redrawing Our Family Tree?* August 1998.

Keyser, Andre. W. *Dawn of Humans. New Finds in South Africa*. May 2000.

Gore, Rick. *Dawn of Humans: People Like Us*. July 2000.

Gore, Rick. *New Find*. August 2002.

Gore, Rick. *The Rise of Mammals*. April 2003.

Websites

National Geographic Society
www.nationalgeographic.com

Institute for Human Origins
www.becominghuman.org

Museum of Paleontology
www.ucmp.berkeley.edu

The Smithsonian Institution
Human Origins Program
www.mnh.si.edu/anthro/humanorigins

National Center for Science Education
www.ncseweb.org

Index

The twin Kennis brothers, artists Alfons (left) and Adrie, reconstruct ancient life.

National Geographic photographer Kenneth Garrett in South Africa with an archaic *Homo sapiens* skull.

One of the world's largest nonprofit scientific and educational organizations, the National Geographic Society was founded in 1888 "for the increase and diffusion of geographic knowledge." Fulfilling this mission, the Society educates and inspires millions every day through its magazines, books, television programs, videos, maps and atlases, research grants, the National Geographic Bee, teacher workshops, and innovative classroom materials. The Society is supported through membership dues, charitable gifts, and income from the sale of its educational products. This support is vital to National Geographic's mission to increase global understanding and promote conservation of our planet through exploration, research, and education.